D1451863

ARCHAIC CLASSICS.

ASSYRIAN GRAMMAR,

AND

READING BOOK.

ARCHAIC CLASSICS.

AN

ELEMENTARY GRAMMAR;

WITH FULL SYLLABARY

AND PROGRESSIVE READING BOOK,

OF

THE ASSYRIAN LANGUAGE,

IN THE CUNEIFORM TYPE.

BY

THE REV. A. H. SAYCE, M.A.,

DEPUTY PROFESSOR OF COMPARATIVE PHILOLOGY, OXFORD.

Author of "An Assyrian Grammar," and "The Principles of Comparative Philology."

Second Edition—Revised and Corrected. .

Wipf and Stock Publishers
EUGENE, OREGON

Wipf and Stock Publishers
199 West 8th Avenue, Suite 3
Eugene, Oregon 97401

Assyrian Grammar
An Elementary Grammar; with Full Syllabary and Progressive Reading Book
By Sayce, A.H.
ISBN: 1-57910-965-9
Publication date: May, 2002
Previously published by Samuel Bagster and Sons, 1875.

TO

THE PRESIDENT AND MEMBERS

OF THE

SOCIETY OF BIBLICAL ARCHÆOLOGY

THIS VOLUME

IS

DEDICATED BY THE AUTHOR.

CONTENTS.

PREFACE TO
THE SECOND EDITION.

A Second Edition must always be gratifying to an author; it is doubly so in the case of a work like the present, which deals in dry outline with a new and struggling study. That an *Elementary Grammar of the Assyrian Language* should have passed through its First Edition in little more than a year, is a welcome sign of hope and promise to those who have at heart the progress of cuneiform research, or the cause of Oriental learning and comparative philology. The present edition has undergone a thorough revision. A few misprints which had unfortunately escaped notice have been corrected, and an additional chapter has been added on Assyrian accentuation, an important but hitherto neglected subject. The syllabary, however, will show the most alteration, every effort having been made to bring it up to the present level of knowledge. In a progressive study like Assyrian, it is true, our acquaintance with the syllabary can never be finally complete until every fragment of inscribed clay has been excavated in Assyria and Babylonia, and subjected to careful examination; nevertheless, each successive year makes our acquaintance with it larger and more certain. Since the syllabary prefixed to this Grammar was first printed, Assyrian literature has been enriched by three important works, the *Assyrische Lesestücke* of Dr. Friedrich Delitzsch, and M. François Lenormant's *Étude sur quelques parties des Syllabaires cunéiformes*, and *Les Syllabaires cunéiformes*. To the latter indefatigable scholar we owe the most systematic attempt yet made to classify and explain the various so-called syllabaries, fragments of which are in the British Museum, and which form the basis of Assyrian decipherment. He has shown that these fall into at least two classes, one of them being intended merely to give a list of the cuneiform characters with their Accadian names. Like the Chinese, the Accadians, it would seem, had classified and named all their characters, dividing them into simple and compound, and a scribe was thus enabled to write from dictation without fear of mistake. Thus No. 1 was called *dil* (Semitised in Assyrian into *dilu*), No. 12 was *muc-muc-nabi* or " muc twice over" (*nabi* for *minnabi*, meaning " twice" in Accadian), the character in question being originally a repetition of that which represented *muc*. The classification was made in the Accadian period, since the names are of Accadian origin and the names assigned to many of the compound characters (No. 12, for instance) can only be explained by reference to their archaic Babylonian forms. Phonetic decay, however, had already attacked the Accadian vocabulary to a great extent, *idu*, for example, which forms part of the name of No. 357, standing for *in-du* "it goes." Initial and even medial sounds were liable to be dropped, but it was the final letters which were most exposed to decay. Words originally different came to have the same form and so to be represented by the same character. Thus ⟩⊢ (primarily a drawing of the tongue) signified " tongue," " voice," " calling," or " assembly," *eme* in Accadian; while ⟩⟶ *me + es*, represented *mes* " many." But both *eme* and *mes* came in course of time to be alike contracted into *me*, and so denoted by the same ideograph. Many allophones are to be explained in a similar way. A foot, for instance, was represented by a hieroglyphic which degenerated into Ⅰ; now " foot " was *essü* in Accadian; but when *essü* became simple *su*, the character which denoted it was interchanged with ⧫ *su* "a hand." Another word for " foot " was *ärig* (for *äri-ga*), literally " the goer," from *ara* " to go." *Duma* also meant " to go," and the idea was expressed by the representation of two legs in the act of walking, which when laid on their side developed into ⧫⟩. *Duma* became successively *duma, dum, dun, dû* and *du*, while *ara* became *ra*, and so ⧫⟩ took the phonetic value of *du*, and the idea of " going " was occasionally represented by ⊨⟩⟩. The Accadians sometimes combined the two characters together, ⊨⟩⟩ ⧫⟩, the second being an unpronounced determinative, and the first pointing out that the word was to be sounded *ra*.

A. H. SAYCE.

PREFACE TO
THE FIRST EDITION.

—⸺—

THE following pages have been written in connection with my lectures upon Assyrian philology, which were commenced in the early part of 1875 under the auspices of the Society of Biblical Archæology, and through the exertions of Mr. W. R. Cooper, the Secretary of the Society. An endeavour has been made for the first time to smooth over the difficulties which beset the entrance to the study of the Assyrian inscriptions, and so attract students to this new and important branch of research. When my "Assyrian Grammar" was published, three years ago, a knowledge of the language was still confined to the few, and there seemed little prospect that the small band of Assyriologues would be much increased for a long while to come. My work was therefore addressed to two classes of readers; to those who were already able to read the inscriptions, and could appreciate a grammar which entered into details and points of scholarship, and to those who were acquainted with the better-known Semitic languages, but wished to learn something of the new dialect which had been so unexpectedly revealed, and promised to throw such a flood of light on Semitic philology in general. The prospect, however, that three years ago seemed so distant has been more than realised. Assyrian has become a "popular" subject; and the world of scholars which once looked with distrust upon the labours of the decipherers, has at last awakened to their interest and importance. Students are flocking in from all sides, and elementary grammars and progressive reading-books, like those which initiate the pupil into Hebrew or Greek, are needed and called for.

The present volume is intended to meet this demand. The cuneiform type which has been freely used throughout will accustom the eye of the reader to the forms of the characters, and as all transliterated words are divided into syllables, even where the Assyrian text is not added, he will be able to reduce them into their original forms. Care has been taken not to burden the memory with unnecessary matter; and practical experience has proved that tabular lists of nouns, verbs, and particles, such as are given in the second part of the book, are the best means for impressing the rudiments of a new language upon the mind. A separate chapter on the syntax has been omitted, since any attempt to enter into details would be inconsistent with the plan of the Grammar, while it has been found more convenient to state those few cases of importance in which Assyrian differs from the syntactical usage of other languages in those places of the accidence to which they naturally belong. The notes appended to each of the reading-lessons are designed to lead the student on to a more advanced and independent acquaintance with the language, and so complete the work of a practical and elementary grammar.

The main difficulty is the Syllabary, the larger part of which will sooner or later have to be learnt by heart. The beginner is advised first to commit to memory the characters which express open syllables, given in pp. 46 and 47, as well as the Determinative Prefixes and Affixes given in p. 48, and then to work at the *monosyllabic* closed syllables. Experience alone can show him what are the commoner and more favourite values with which a character is used; and he must be content to be continually a learner, keeping the Syllabary constantly at his side for purposes of reference, and remembering that any endeavour to learn the *whole* Syllabary is a needless and useless task.   He will soon come to know what characters and what values are most frequently employed, and what ideographs are most likely to occur in the inscriptions.

The hieroglyphic origin of the Syllabary, and its adaptation to the wants of a foreign language, will give the key to many of the difficulties he will meet with.   Its Accadian inventors spoke an agglutinative dialect; and each hieroglyphic, which in course of time came to be corrupted into a cuneiform character (like the modern Chinese), originally expressed the sound of the word denoting the object or idea for which it stood.   The same picture could stand for more ideas than one, and might therefore be pronounced in more than one way, so that when the Semitic Assyrians (or rather Babylonians) borrowed the cuneiform system of writing, using what were words in Accadian as mere phonetic values, polyphony became inevitable, and the same character represented several phonetic powers.   Even in Accadian the characters could be employed phonetically as well as ideographically; and the Assyrians, while turning the dictionary of the Accadians into a huge syllabary, did not forget the hieroglyphic origin of the writing, but reserved to themselves the power of using a character not only as the representative of a syllabic sound, but also as an ideograph to which of course a Semitic pronunciation was attached.

Many of the characters exhibit their primitive form at the first glance; ⟑ for instance, clearly standing for " the tongue of a balance."   In other cases the resemblance to the objects originally signified is not very visible in the simplified forms of the characters as used in Assyria, and we have to go back to the archaic Babylonian type to detect the likeness.   Thus ⟑ has lost all resemblance to "the sun;" and it is not until we remember the archaic ⟚ that we discover the circle which stood for the great luminary of day.   A large number of characters are compound, and when they are used ideographically their meaning can often be determined by considering what is the meaning of the separate characters of which they are made up. Thus ⟨cuneiform⟩ is "a mouth," and ⟨cuneiform⟩ "a drop of water;" the compound ⟨cuneiform⟩ therefore naturally denotes the act of "drinking." So, again, the Assyrian ⟨cuneiform⟩ "a month" is the simplified form of the archaic ⟨cuneiform⟩, where ⟨cuneiform⟩ the numeral 30 (expressing the 30 days of the month), is placed within the circle of the sun.

The use of polyphones no doubt increases the difficulty of decipherment, but the student will find that practically it is not so embarrassing as it would seem at first sight to be. The Assyrians intended their inscriptions to be read (at all events except in the case of texts like those of the astrological tablets, which were addressed to the initiated only), and accordingly adopted all possible means of obviating the disadvantages of a polyphonic system of writing. The following rules should be observed by the student in selecting one of the many values a given character may bear :—

(1) The existence of an ideograph should never be assumed, unless it is indicated by a phonetic complement, or unless the inscription (like the astrological ones generally) is written throughout ideographically rather than phonetically.

(2) Where two characters come together (such as *ca* and *ac*), the first of which ends with the same vowel as that with which the second begins, we may infer that they form one closed syllable (as *cac*).

(3) If a character expresses an open syllable (as *ri*) as well as a closed one (as *tal*), the open is to be preferred to the closed (unless contra-indicated).

(4) Those values are to be selected which offer a triliteral (or biliteral) root, and not a pluriliteral one.

(5) Notice must be taken of the final or initial consonant of the character which precedes or follows the one we are considering, as the Assyrians frequently doubled a consonant to show what value is to be chosen in a doubtful case. Thus ⌐𝕀𝕀𝕀 𝕀⌐𝕖𝕀 must be read *dan-nin*, as *dan* alone out of the many possible values of the first character ends with *n*.

(6) A character which denotes a syllable beginning with a vowel is very rarely used after one which ends with a consonant.

(7) Words and lines end together, and proper names, &c., are pointed out by Determinative Prefixes and Affixes.

(8) Variant readings and variant forms of the same root must be carefully observed, as they often decide the pronunciation of a word where all other means fail.

(9) Experience will show that common use had set apart one or two values of a given character which were preferably employed to all others.

(10) Those values must be adopted which bring out a correct grammatical form, or enable us to compare the Assyrian word (should the context determine its meaning) with a similar root in the cognate languages.

It is not so much the existence of polyphones, however, that forms the chief defect in the Assyrian mode of writing. The phonology of the inventors of the writing was not the same as the phonology of the Assyrians, and sounds which were distinct in Assyrian had to be represented by one and the same sign. ⌐𝕀𝕀𝕀⌐ is both *hu* or *u* (הו and א and ו) and *yu* (יו), 𝕀𝕀 *za* and *tsa*, ⌐⌐𝕀𝕀 *da* and *dha*, ⟨𝕀⌐𝕀 *di* and *dhi*, ⌐𝕀𝕀 *e* (ע) and a modified י, ⤮⤮⤚ *bu* and *pu*. Similarly the same characters denoted both *m* and *v*, and no distinction was made between final *d*, *dh*, and *t*; *b* and *p*; *g*, *c*, and *k*; and *z*, *ś*, *ts*, and even *s*; while closed syllables might begin as well as end with any of these doubtful letters. The uncertainty which results from this as to the initial or final letter of a syllable would naturally not press upon the Assyrian; but it is the main difficulty against which the modern decipherer has to contend, and can only be overcome by the examination of new texts and the comparison of numerous passages.

A. H. SAYCE.

Queen's College, Oxford, April, 1875.

ASSYRIAN GRAMMAR.

SYLLABARY.

The characters of the Assyrian Syllabary were originally hieroglyphics, representing objects and ideas. The words by which these were denoted in the Turanian language of the Accadian inventors of the cuneiform system of writing became phonetic sounds when it was borrowed by the Semitic Assyrians, though the characters could still be used ideographically as well as phonetically. When used ideographically the pronunciation was, of course, that of the Assyrians.

In the following table only the forms of the characters found on the majority of the Assyrian monuments are given. Sometimes the so-called Hieratic characters were employed (*e.g.*, in the Cyprian Stele of Sargon) which differ but slightly from the Babylonian. Ancient Babylonian varied again in the forms of several characters. The Elamite or Susianian characters have the same form as the ancient Babylonian, while the Protomedic are modified from the Assyrian.

The Assyrian word in the right-hand column is a translation of the Accadian word (used in Assyrian as a phonetic value) in the left-hand column, and was the sound given to the character in the Assyrian inscriptions whenever it was read as an ideograph.

Phonetic Value (Accadian word).	Cuneiform Character.	Assyrian rendering.	Meaning.
1. as	➤	magaru, dilu ...	*obedient* (*happy*)
ruv (rum, ru)	,,	zicaru, dilu	*a memorial*
dil	,,	nabu, dilu	*to proclaim*, name of the
	,,	estin, khidu, edisu ...	*one* [character
	,,	namkullū	*?*
ina (*Ass. value*)	,,	ina	*in*
	,,	Assur (*an abbreviation*)	*Assyria*
† kharra ...	,,	samu, tuhamtu ...	*heaven, the deep*
	,,	nadanu	*to give*

2

Phonetic Value (Accadian word).	Cuneiform Character.	Assyrian rendering.	Meaning.
2. khal	►►	nacaśu, buligu ...	*to cut, division*
khas	,,	khasu	name of the character
khal	,,	gararu	*to roll stormily*
	,,	pulukhu	*reverence*
	,,	zuzu...	*a fixture*
3. ?	►►►	[sumunesrit] ...	*eighteen* (Oppert *"fifteen"*)
4. an, †ana ...	►►⊢	sakū, samū, ilu, Anu,	*high, sky, god, the god Anu*
†anna, †annab	,,	sakū, samū, ilu, Anu,	*high, sky, god, the god Anu*
†dimir, †dingir	,,	ilu	*god*
śa	,,	cacabu	*star*
†essa	,,	ilutu sa sibri ...	*divinity of corn*
an	,,	supultu, rēsu ...	*ear of corn, head*
4*a*. nab (*see* 168)		nabbu	*divinity*
4*b*. simidan ...		nalbar-same... ...	*the zenith*
4*c*. alat, alap ...		sēdu	*spirit* (*divine bull*)
4*d*. lamma ...		lamaśśu	*colossus*
alat	,,	buhidu	*colossus*
5. khaz (khas, khats)	►⊱	nadu, nacaśu ...	*to place, to cut*
kut (kud) ...	,,	nacaśu, gazaru ...	*to cut, to cut*
tar	,,	nacaśu, danu, sāmu	*to cut, to judge, to set* (*determine*)
sil (śil, śila) ...	,,	sūku, panu	*canal, before*
gug, †citamma	,,		
	,,	sallatu, halacu, eribu	*spoil, to go, to descend* (*flow*)
6. pal	►⊱Y⊰	ebiru, etiku, palu,	*to cross, to pass through, time*
		napalcutu, nucuru,	*or year, to revolt, enemy,*
		palu	*sword*
tal	,,	ebiru, etiku	*to cross, to pass through*
pal	,,	supilu sa sinnis,	*sexual part of a woman,*
		pukhkhu sa sinnis,	*sexual part of a woman,*
		supiltu, pilakku	*the lower part, an axe*
nuk (?) ...	,,	nakū...	*to sacrifice*
†zabur... ...	,,	admu, akhri, khiru ...	*man, behind, lord*

Phonetic Value (Accadian word).	Cuneiform Character.	Assyrian rendering.	Meaning.
7. bat, be ...		pagru, pitu, mutu, labiru, uduntu	*corpse, to open, to die, old, quantity*
til, †badhdhu	,,	gamaru, pagru, katu	*complete, corpse, hand*
us	,,	dāmu	*blood (offspring)*
†khar	,,		
ziz(?),mit,†idim	,,		
	,,	nakbu, samu, captu, belu, enuva, tsēru	*channel, heaven, heavy, lord, when, desert*
8. lugud ...		sarcu	*white race*
9. adama ...		adamatu	*black (red) race*
10. susru... ...		ussusu	*destruction (surname of Anu)*
11. gir		sumuk-same, padhru	*vault of heaven, to strike*
rum	,,	littu, padhru ...	*sword, point*
gir	,,	girū, zukakibu, pad-anu, birku	*scorpion, plough, lightning*
at, adh ...			
12. pur, pul ...		passaru	*to explain* (?)
du, gim ...	,,	edissu, sumnu ...	*alone, fat*
‡mucmuc-nabi (see 107a)	,,		
†usu	,,	edisu	*solitary*
	,,	basmu, butu, macaru, garru	*sweet odour, desert (?), to sell, or exchange, expedition* (?)
13. kur		naciru, sannu, pappu	*to change, enemy,* name of ch.
pap	,,	pappu, zicaru, tarbu, natsaru, akhu	name, *male, young man, to defend, brother*
13a. *khal,‡dili-dili-nabi ("dil twice")		muttallicu	*passenger, sick*
‡gisi-u-khallacu ("joined to the sign khal")	,,	pusku	*difficult*
14. utuci... ...		samsu	*the Sun*
15. zubu... ...		gamlu	*benefit*
gam	,,	sicru...	*kindness*
16. taltal... ...		Ea	*the god Hea*

2*

Phonetic Value (Accadian word).	Cuneiform Character.	Assyrian rendering.	Meaning.
17. zicura ...		citim	*lower* or *beneath*
18. cit, †cuda, se ...		epikhu, carasu ...	*to blow, property (standard, camp)*
†śabura ...	,,	calū, patā	*the whole, to open*
†gudibir ...	,,	cupkhu	?
tak	,,	Maruducu	*Merodach*
	,,	ezibu	*to leave*
19. seslam ...		cipratu	*race* or *region*
20. ka, †gita ...		... ...	determinative of measure
21. cit (kit, cat) ...		salamu	*to accomplish*
22. ru, sub ...		nadu, nadanu, takku, raddu, cabadu, pakadu, arcat	*to present, to give, ?, to add, to oppress* or *be multitudinous, to oversee, after*
u, ub, bu ...	,,	iśbu	*evening*
23. mu		sumu, santu, zicaru, nadanu, ya, samu	*name, year, memorial, to give, my, sky*
	,,	masaddu, cu'aśu, khalacu, cuśśu, vācu	*?, ?, ?, throne, ?*
†nurma ...	,,		
23a. ?		idlutu	*heroism*
24. nu		la, (ul), tsalamu, rubu	*not, image, prince*
†pateśi ...	,,	zicaru	*male (viceroy)*
25. kul (*Assyrian value* zir)		ziru	*seed (offspring)*
26. zir		nūru...	*light (meteor)*
27. na		zicaru, annu, samu, makhirtu, rubu	*male, this, sky, front, prince*
28. ti, til, tsil ...		baladhu, napistu, naśu lakū, tsabatu, dakhu usibu, dapanu-sa-rucubi, anbu, tsilu	*life, life, to raise to take, to seize, to face dwell, side* (or *wheel) of a chariot, ?, side*

Phonetic Value (Accadian word).	Cuneiform Character.	Assyrian rendering.	Meaning.
29. uru, eri ...	𒌷	ālu	*a city (tent)*
30. uru	𒌷	ālu, abubu	*city, heap of corn*
31. erim	𒌷	isittu	*a foundation*
32. sek	𒌷	sakummatu	*a summit*
33. gur	𒌷	caśamu	*?*
34. sacir, saciśa ...	𒌷	... ...	*?*
35. ukki	𒌷	uku, pukhru ...	*people, assembly*
36. uru,†gisgal ...	𒌷	ālu, manzazu ...	*city, fortress*
mulu	„	nisu	*man*
37. silik	𒌷	sagaburu	*strong protector, rank*
38. banśur ... (See No. 197*b*.)	𒌷	passuru	Lenormant *"kind of parasol," dish*
38*a*. kal, gar ...	𒌷	?	*?*
39. ca, gu, cir, †du, †zu, †cagu ... (See No. 331.) pi (*Ass. value*)	𒅗	pū, amatu, appu,pānu, inu, uznu, bunnu, makhru, sepu, amaru, amanu, kābu, sāsu,ricmu,sagamu, cibu, mātu,adilu	*mouth, fealty, face, face, eye, ear, form, front, foot, sight, completion, to speak, ?, push, ?, mass, country (properly face of the country), ?*
duk	„	ilu sa napkhari, erisu	*god of the universe, to ask*
gu,†cagu ...	„	calu, saku - sa - me, canicu, cagamu	*all, drinking of water, seal, ?*
ca ... ... śak	„	ricim, sunnu, idculu śangu	*blow, a half, confidence (?)* ?
39*a*. duddhu ...	𒅗 𒅗	dabibu, pālu, idacculu	*deviser, ?, ?*
39*b*. gude ...	𒅗	nabu, khababu, nagagu	*proclaimer, lover (?), ?*
39*c*. śidi, śiśi ...	𒅗	urrikhtu	*?*

Phonetic Value (Accadian word).	Cuneiform Character.	Assyrian rendering.	Meaning.
39*d.* cimmu ...		sipru, dhemu ...	*explanation, law*
40. me		takhatsu	*battle*
41. impar ...		... ...	*glory (name)*
42. emi		lisānu	*tongue (language)*
43. ?		saptu	*lip (sentence)*
44. ?		saptu, tsumu ...	*lip, thirst*
45. ?		tsumu	*thirst (fast)*
46. cu		acalu, khadhdhu ...	*to eat, food* (חנט)
47. mû		camu	*to burn* (?)
48. ?		pukhkhu	*the breath*
49. ?		tsalamtu	*darkness*
50. ibira		damkaru (*of Acc. origin*)	?
51. ?		ikhimu	*he burnt (devoured)*
51*a.* ?		?	?
52. ?		?	?
53. ?		?	?
54. bat		imtu ...	*poison (philtre)*
55. ?		?	*terror*
56. ?		?	?
57. nak		satu	*to drink*
58. ?		uru	*city*
59. la		laluru, khazbu ...	?, ?

Phonetic Value (Accadian word).	Cuneiform Character.	Assyrian rendering.	Meaning.
60. tu … …	⟪cuneiform⟫	eribu, śummatu …	to descend or enter or set (of the Sun), dove
†turi,†tura …	„	eribu, murtsu …	to descend, &c., sickness
61. li … …	⟪cuneiform⟫ (note these variant forms)	rāmu,liliśu … …	high, ?
gub, gu …	„	illu … … …	high or precious (הלל)
ni … …	„		
62. apin, pin, uru	⟪cuneiform⟫	epinu, ussu … …	foundation (city)
†engar …	„	iccaru	ground (digging, root)
63. makh …	⟪cuneiform⟫	tsiru, makhkhu (from Acc.), rubū, mahdu	supreme, supreme, great, much
	„	bahalu, tublu, tizkaru	prince (?), sovereign (?), ?
64. bar, mas … par, maś	⟪cuneiform⟫	paratsu, burru, bāru, usuru, tsindu, akhratu, akhkhuru, tsātu, rikātu, akhatu, akhu, akhitu, arcu, tsabiu, cimtu, ukku	to divide, half, half, bound, to bind, another, after, future, future, a second, brother, other, after, gazelle, family, people
	„	camātu, gabbi, tinū, enitu, pisaktu, cabitu, mala, palaśu, tuhāmu, zibtu, dallu, ciśittu, niśu, ruzzu, elitu, śanku, makhazu, eru, asaridu, pulu, maru, eramu, ibbu, libutu, amaru, masū, vassaru, zumru, cabadtu	heap (?), all, ?, ?, oracle, much, as many as, to weigh, ?, ?, the Tigris, ?,?,?, upper, chain, battle, to beget, eldest, cattle, son, offspring, white, whiteness, to see, ?, to abandon, body, the liver
mas … …	„	māsu, Adaru, asibu, ellu, tsabatu, māzusa-ecili	?, the god Adar, to dwell, high (precious), to take, burning (?) of a field
śa … …	„		
65. rat, sit …	⟪cuneiform⟫	radhu … …	an arc

Phonetic Value (Accadian word).	Cuneiform Character.	Assyrian rendering.	Meaning.
66. nun	![char]	rubū, rabu, nunu, (*fr. Acc.*)	*prince, great, prince*
zil, śil, †humis, khan (?)	"		
66a. asagara ...	![char]	asagaru	*a hurricane*
67. tur	![char]	tarbatsu	*rest* or *eclipse* (Op. "*meridian*")
68. silam ...	![char]	littu...	*offspring*
68a. akar ...	![char]	aplukhtu	*reverence*
69. biru (*perhaps Ass.*)	![char]	suttu, uritsu, tsiptu, nipikhu	*dream, offspring, product, revenue*
70. cun, gun ...	![char]	zibbatu, zumbu ...	*tail, tail*
71. ?	![char]	?	?
72. ?	![char]	?	?
73. khu, pak (bag)	![char]	itstsuru, śaru ...	*bird, king* (?)
khu,pak,†musen	"	musennu	*bird*
74. pacac ...	![char]	ciribu, sumelu ...	*middle, left hand*
75. śa	![char]	nabū	*to proclaim*
76. ik	![char]	iku (*or* ikku), daltu, khamdhu,patu,nukh-su, nāru, nallabu	*door, quick journey, to open, prosperity, river, ?*
gal	"	basū, sacunu, nasu, labinu, saku, diku	*to be, placed, to raise, brick, high, slain*
mal			
gal	"	ikku, rutstsunu, malū, asabu, pitū, cānu, natsaru, pasakhu	*?, to fill, to dwell, to open, to establish, to defend, ?*
77. tsim, zim, nam (*Acc. prefix of abstract noun*)	![char]	simtu, sakhalu ...	*destiny, plague* (?)
		śinuntu	*a swallow*
nam	"	nabu, śimmu ...	*to proclaim, destiny* (*plague*)
ram	"	pikhatu, lā	*a governor, not*
		annu	*this*
77a. ?	![char]	?	*insect*

Phonetic Value (Accadian word).	Cuneiform Character.	Assyrian rendering.	Meaning.
78. pak (?) ...		itstsuru, aribu ...	*a bird, locust*
79. mut		banū, da'mu, uppu, aladu, icbu, biśru, barradu (paradu)	*to create, obscure, ?, to bear children, ?, flesh, seed*
‡musen-dugū, ("good bird")	„	banu-sa-aladi	*creator of family*
80. zi		napistu, nisu, pilū, naśakhu, dikū, būā, saparu	*life (soul), man (spirit), work, to take away, smitten, to come, to send*
81. gi, śa... ...		kanū, duppu-sadhru, simtu, zicaru, mātu, eśiri, tāru, gimiru, pudak, cunu	*reed, written tablet, foundation, memorandum, country, bands, to restore, all, ?, established*
81a. caradin ...		cissu	*multitudinous*
82. ?		?	*?*
83. ri, tal, dal ...		tallu, ramū, lilu, tsakku, paraśu - sa - rikhuti, parsidu, zēnu, rihu	*name of character, height, ?, ?, ?, to fly away, ?, ?*
di	„	nabadhu	*brilliance*
es	„	nadū	*brightness (of a star)*
sa	„	saruru	*the firmament*
84. gub, cab (kap)		sumelu	*left hand*
kat	„	gubbu (of Accadian origin)	*left hand*
85. tun, khub ...		khatu	*?*
86. pulug ...		carasu-sa-etsi ...	*implement of wood*
87. ac, gar ...		episu, banū, makharu, nabu, Nabū, khaśiśu, pit-uzni, rapsa-uzni, khubbu-sakani, takhazu	*to make, to build, to be present, to proclaim, Nebo, the intelligent, the opener of the ears, the enlarger of the ears, hollow of a reed, battle*
ac	„	belu, pitsu	*lord, white*
88. me ...		takhatsu	*battle*
89. sus		?	*?*

Phonetic Value (Accadian word).	Cuneiform Character.	Assyrian rendering.	Meaning.
90. ?		?	?
91. cum, kum ... kad		citu	*linen*
91*a*. *sa		gallabu	*sleeve* (?)
91*b*. sinik ...		bīnu...	?
92. ? ... ... ?		tsupuru ... ... simmu	*nail* (*nail-mark*) *settlement*
92*a*. ?		kharru	?
92*b*. sacil ...		cillu...	?
92*c*. dubbin, ‡gada-taccuru		tsupru, masaru, tsum-bu, ubanu, imdhu	*nail, to leave* (?), *tail* (?), *peak* (*thumb*), *staff* (?)
93. dim, tim, tiv, tī		ricśu, riciś-kanē, mar-caśu, timmu	*bond, bundle of reeds, cable, name of the character*
94. mun (munu)...		dhabtu	*benefit*
95. pulug (*from Assn.*)		pulugu	*division* or *choice*
95*a*. ?		eribu	*descent*
96. en ... ... †enu		belu, enu ... ... adi ... ... samu	*lord, lord* *up to* *sky*
97. dara		turakhu ... ... Ea	*antilope* *the god Ea*
98. mu		sumu, inbu	*name, fruit*
99. sur (zur) ...		zamaru, zarakhu, tsar-uru, naśakhu-sa-amati, ridu, khabsu, capalu, zunnu, sum-ma, basu	*to make go forth, to rise, illumination, removal of fealty, servant, trodden down* (?), *?, rain, thus, to exist*
100. sukh (śukh)		pultu, mātu, naparcu, zimu, pallu, nasaku, tihamtu	*?, country, to break, glory, ?, to climb, the deep*
†tiskhu ...		ramcuti	*herd* [or *stay* ?]

Phonetic Value (Accadian word).	Cuneiform Character.	Assyrian rendering.	Meaning.
101. śucus ...		Istar...	the goddess Istar
102. se,sakh(śakh), nakh, nikh		surbu	prince
		paśakhu	to pass over
103. ba		episu, banū, zuzu, ciśu, nasaru, esiru, su, pitu	to make, to create, to fix, a sword, ?, a shrine, he, to open
104. zu, la ...		lamadu, idū, mudu, ca, nindanu	to learn, to know, wise, thy, a gift
104a. abzu ...		absū	the abyss
105. śu, sir ..		zumuru, tsuru, masacu, rabā, rādū	a body, ?, skin, increase, to add
106. sun (śun) ...		gablu, takhazu ...	front (middle, battle), battle
107. muk ...		muccu	a building
107a ‡mukmuk-nabi ("muk twice")		basmu	altar of incense
108. zadim ...		śaśinu	plant (Heb. םכס)
109. nit (nitakh, nita), eri		zicaru, ardu... ...	man, slave
110. idu, itu, iti ...		arkhu, tsit-arkhi ...	month, exit of month
111. sakh, sukh ...		damaku, dabu, sakhu	prosperous, a bear, name of character
112. sibir... ...		sibru, kharpu ...	corn, crop
113. gur		tāru, śacibu, basu, nacru-sa-amati	to restore, ?, to be (become), breaker of faith
114. dar		tarru, birmi, atsu ...	?, variegated cloths, growth
dar, ‡śī-gunū ("śi with additions")	,,	litu, sutruru, pitsu ...	offspring, white, white
115. ?		dispu	honey

Phonetic Value (Accadian word).	Cuneiform Character.	Assyrian rendering.	Meaning.
116. śa, pa ...		kurnu, masadu, markaśu, bu'anu	?, ?, firmament (bond), ulcer
[‡śa-gitu] ...	,,		
117. gis (?) ...		samu	the sky
118. śi		karnu, malu, giru, enisu, śamu, issaccu, dussu, itanu, pitu, cunnu, samu	horn, to fill, enemy (or campaign), man, blue, prince, ?, ?, to open, established, sky
śig	,,	malū...	to fill (give)
118a. śicca ...		atudu	he-goat
119. śa'ib ...		'urukhkhu	road (?)
120. śi (śe) (sometimes confused with dar) gun		gunnu, calu, pilū, pilutu, eru, atsu-sa-etsi-u-kani	garden, entrails (kidneys), choice, choice, to beget, growth of trees and grass
121. mā		elippu	a ship
122. uz, mus ...		enzu...	goats' hair cloth
123. ** ur ...		calū naccalu ...	a complete vessel
124. ticul, dellu ... dimśun		sukkullu, acū ...	intelligence, ?
125. surru ...		surrū, calū ...	beginning (?), vessel
126. guana ...		kablu	middle
127. ?		eratu	pregnant
128. dir		adru, khalabu, sutruru, khibu, mikid-isati	dark, covered, covered, wanting, burning of fire
śa	,,	śamu	blue
pir	,,	saku-sa-nisi	head of a man
dak	,,	nikhabbu, malu, ikubbu	covering, to fill, vault
129. maś, (alat)		tsabu, alapu ...	soldier, warrior spirit (bull)

Phonetic Value (Accadian word).	Cuneiform Character.	Assyrian rendering.	Meaning.
130. sak (ris *in Ass.*)		risu, karnu, śangu, panu, rabu, avilu, pukhu	*head, horn, chain, face, great, man,* ?
130*a.* sakus ...		saku-sa-risi, asaridu... caivanu	*top of the head, eldest the planet Saturn*
130*b.* eśśat ...		?	?
131. mukh ...		mukhkhu	*brain*
132. ?		?	?
133. uru		zicaru	*male*
134. aru		nestu	*female*
135. gudhu ...		karradu	*hero*
136. can		adaru, adirtu ...	*dark, eclipse*
137. tab (tap,dhab)		tsabatu, tamakhu, etsibu, sitenu, uraddu, tabbu, khamadhu	*to seize, to hold, to establish, double* (?), *to add* (*give back*), *double, swift*
‡ dili-dili-nabi ("*dil twice*")	"	surru, napkharu ...	*beginning, totality*
138. (u)cū · ...		kurku	?
138. rū (ra) ...		banu, daltu	*to make, a door*
kak	"	episu, cala, dāru ...	*to make, all, to endure*
	"	siccatu, rapdu ...	*door* (?), ?
dū, gag (*sometimes in Ass.* cal)	"	banu, danu ...	*to create, to judge*
139. ni, ne ...		yahu [*or i*]	name of the character
zal (zalli), ili	"	yahu...	name of the character
i	"	akhkhuru, namaru, masu, zicaru, azalu, narabu, nākhu, sunku-sa-bissati, ciśallu	*presence, to see, week* (?), *man, to depart,* ?, *to rest* (?), *want of* *, *altar*
140. ili ... ... ‡i-minnabi ("*i twice*")		?	?
141. ir		salalu	*to spoil*
†sucal ...	"	sucallu	*fruit*

Phonetic Value (Accadian word).	Cuneiform Character.	Assyrian rendering.	Meaning.
142. mal, ma, e ... gal, gā, †piśannu		bitu, sacanu ...	house, to establish
†ilba ...	"	saracu, maru, callu ...	to give, young, to restrain
143. gusur ...		gusuru, idlu, nuru ...	beam, hero, light
144. cisal ...		ciśallu	altar
145. ?		?	?
146. nen, †lucu, †ekhi †damalla, †dagal		ummu ... ... rapsu ... ... taci	mother large ?
147. ?		ummu	mother
148. gapi... ...		? ... ... ?	
149. ?		alittu	generatrix
150. ega		agu	crown
151. ?		remu	mercy
152. ?		remu	grace
153. gan (gana) †gāgunū		iclu, padanu, ginu, nabadhu	field, plain, enclosure (garden), light
†gāgunū ...	"	khaśaśu	intelligent (to determine)
car	"	sapalu, caru... ...	lower, fortress
†aganateti ...	"	nasū...	to raise
154. dak... ...		napaldhu, rapadu, tāru	to survive, ?, to restore
bara (par) ...	"	sutruru, adannu ...	covered, a season
155. ciśim, cisi, zibin, surin, sarin		ciśimmu, nabbillu, tsatsiru, sīkhu	different kinds of locusts
kharub (from Ass.)	"	kharubu, zirbabu ...	a locust, do.
156. agan, ubir ...		tulu, tsirtu	worm, snake
157. amas, śubura		śuburu	a feast

Phonetic Value (Accadian word).	Cuneiform Character.	Assyrian rendering.	Meaning.
158. us, † nita, † nitakh, † dhūcus, gis ...		emidu, zicaru, ridu, mutstsu, nitakhu, isaru, rikhu, abadu	to stand, man, servant, offspring, man, phallus, smell(?), ?
159. kas		sinātu	urine
160. tak		abnu, saku-sa-icli ...	stone, top of a field
161. tik, gū ...		makhru, mekhitstu, cisadu, mātu, napkharu, akhu	front, battle, neighbourhood (bank, neck), country, totality, side (bank)
161a. giscun ...		etsen-tsiru	tip of the tail
161b. muśub ...		nasu-sa-resi, saku-sa-resi	lifting of the head, top of the head
162. gun		biltu	tribute (a talent)
163. dhur (dur) ...		karnu	a crescent
164. ?		eru	copper
165. hubisega ...		Bilu	Bel
166. sana (sa) (read irba in Ass.)		irbu	four
167. ab (ap, abba) es	"	abtu, esu, tamtu ... bitu, kabu	?, ?, the sea house, hollow (?)
168. nab (nap) (see 4a)		nuru	light
169. mul, †ana-essecu ("ana three times") ...		caccabu, nabadhu ...	star, brightness
170. tak (tag), sum, nas sum ... ... tak, †suridu ...	" "	labanu, libitu, lapatu, bāru, naclu dabakhu ... ... zuhunu, labatsu, makhatsu - sa - ali, śalatsu, bāru, sālu, nabatsu, nadu itpukh	brick, omen, hinge, lake (?), complete to cut the throat (sacrifice) splendour, spectre, stronghold of a city, ?, lake (?), ?, ?, situated he strangled

Phonetic Value (Accadian word).	Cuneiform Character.	Assyrian rendering.	Meaning.
171. cā		bābu	gate
172. az (ats, aś) ...		atsu	name of the character
173. uk (ug) ...		udmu [or tammu], ucu	man [or paragon], great (?)
174. um, mus ... dikh ... dub, dib (duppa)		ummu, lību, dabacu abnu, canacu-sa-abni lāvu, dippu, tsabatu, lavū, sapacu, tabacu, saraku, tuppu, tsipu	?, to cleave to stone, signet tablet, document, to seize, to approach, to heap up, to heap up, to be red (?), ?, produce (?)
175. śumuk ...		sūtu	library (?)
176. śamak ...		mutstsatu	library
177. urud (urudu)		eru	bronze
178. Ninā ...		Ninua	Nineveh (literally fish-town)
179. i, ‡i-gittū ("i extended") khi		nahidu, naku, atsu-sa-samsi khu	clear (glorious), pure, sunrise glorious (?)
180. gan, can (kan) khi ... ... kam ...		annu, nagabu, basu, su, khagalu, aladu *	cloud, canal, to be, he (this), to irrigate, to beget forms ordinal numbers
181. ad (at) ...		abu	father (king)
182. tsi		martu	body
183. ya		naku	pure
184. tur ... ... dū (dumu) ...		zakhru, maru, karradu ablu, maru	small, young, young warrior son, son
185. ginna, khibiz		muniru	overwhelmer (commander)
186. ibila (borrowed from Ass.)		ablu...	son

Phonetic Value (Accadian word).	Cuneiform Character.	Assyrian rendering.	Meaning.
187. turrak (?) ...		bintu, martu ...	*daughter, woman*
188. turrak (?) ...		bintu	*daughter*
189. dumugu ... agu, acu ...		sinu	*the moon-god*
190. ta, nas (*See* 205)		ina, ultu ... ... minā	*in, from* *why?*
191. ?		iclitu, edhutu ...	*darkness (prison), darkness*
192. in		innu, biltu, silu, pillu	name of ch., *mastery, rock* (?), [*judge*
193. †un-gal, †lugal sar (*borrowed from Ass.*)		sarru, saru	*king, monarch*
194. rab, raba (rap) dim... ...	 ,,	rabbu	*?*
195. dim, dimma		macutu, lamastu, ulalu	*feebleness, a phantom, spirit (whence the month* Elul*)*
196. cib, (cip, kip)		?	?
197. bi, cas (kas), ul cas	 ,,	sane, sannu, su, suātu, nakbu cāsu (*borrowed fr. Ac.*) sicaru, carpatu	*two, second, he, this, channel* *double, beer, a cup*
197*a*. kharran ...		khammu	*a quarter of the sky (point of the compass)*
197*b*. sucit (?) ...		passuru	*dish*
198. ?		kharatsu	*to make*
199. cas (kas), ras †kharran ... †cas-cal ...	 ,, ,,	kharranu (durgu), sane, rabadhu kharranu (*from Acc.*)	*road, two,* ? *road*
200. illat... ...		illat	*army*
201. suptu (*from Ass.*)		suptu	*troops (watch)*

Phonetic Value (Accadian word).	Cuneiform Character.	Assyrian rendering.	Meaning.
202. gur		namandu	*measure* (?)
†ninda ...	„	ittū	*a sign*
203. ? ... ... (*See No.* 138.)		?	" *abundance, generosity* " (Le normant)
204. is (iśi), mil, mis		sadu, urru	*mountain* (*heap*), *light*
†śakhar ...	,	'ipru, bisśatu ...	*dust, mud*
	„	summa	*thus* (*if*)
205. ? (*See* 190)		?	" *to begin* " (Lenormant)
206. rim, cabar, im		sulū, sanu(tu) ...	*mound, second* (?)
		eribu	*to descend*
207. sim, rik,†śiriz		sammu	*price* (*income*)
208. ?		?	?
208. ?		nacmu	*a captive*
209. ku, kum, ri ...		saku, khasalu ...	*top, to destroy*
210. ur		isittu, cipśu-sa-nisi, uzunu, udlu, śunu, urcitu	*foundation* (*the nadir*), *sole of the foot, equal weight, level ground,* ?, *plummet*
211. il,†cacaśiga ...		?	?
212. du (dun) ...		alacu, alacu-khamdhu, tabalu - khamdhu, licu - khamdhu, alacu-maru	*to go, a swift journey, a swift onset, a swift march, a little journey*
gub (kup) ...	„	nazazu	*to fix* (*to wax of the moon*)
gin,‡aragubbū	„	nazuzu, basu, alacu, cānu, saparu, magaru, anacu	*to be fixed, to exist, to go, to establish, to send, to love, 1*
sa, ra, ir,†gubba	„	aragubbū	*name of the character*
		tsabatu, sapiru, calu, sulū	*to seize, messenger, all, mound*

Phonetic Value (Accadian word).	Cuneiform Character.	Assyrian rendering.	Meaning.
212a. ‡aradudu-nabi ("*ara or gub twice*")		cānu, uzuzu, ceśu-sa-elappi, alacu-sa-cissati	*to establish, fix, pain of the womb, marching of a multitude*
213. gum, nitakh		rabu, nisu	*an official, a man*
214. **r		?	*" to adhere"* (Lenormant)
215. rim		iśdu, sulu	*foundation, heap*
216. rik, khil ...		?	?
217. gesdin (" *tree of life*")		caranu, curunnu ...	*vine, wine*
218. ib (ip) ...		gablu, su, agagu, nakamu	*middle, he, anger, to be angry*
tum (tuv, tu)	„	khardatu	*fear*
‡ urugal, ‡arali	„	mitu...	*death* (*Hades*)
219. egir..: ...		arcu (arcatu) ...	*after*
aba	„		
220. paz (?) ...		'imiru	*beast* (*ass*), *homer* (*a measure*)
221. gis, nen (?)...		etsu, zicaru, rabu, esiru, atta	*tree* (*wood*), *memorandum, great, temple, thou*
iz (itz, iś) (*Ass. value*)	„		
gis	„	samu	*heaven*
221a. gudhu ...		caccu, tugultu, bilu, gudhu	*weapon, service* (*servant*), *lord, end*
221b. alal ...		alallu, miśu, metsu ...	*papyrus, pure* (?), *shoot* (?)
222. pa, du (?) ...		aru, gappu, gisdaru...	*fibre, wing, sceptre*
khut, khat, cun	„	nahru-sa-yumi ...	*dayspring*
222a. luga		surupu, mikhitsu ...	*burnt, ulcer*
222l. gistar, tirtar		tirtu, śuśaccu ...	*form* (*body*), ?
223. pu		*graphic variant of sign*	

Phonetic Value (Accadian word).	Cuneiform Character.	Assyrian rendering.	Meaning.
224. mar, nikh ...	𒈥	marru, sacanu, migganu, pada, radu, basu	*path, to establish, enclosure, ?, descent, to exist*
225. ge, cit ...	𒄀	citu, zacicu	*below, abyss*
lil	,,	cītu	*below*
226. hu (u), sam	𒄷	umu, ammatu ...	*the same, a cubit*
†cus	,,	akhu, acalu	*brother (?), to eat*
227. ga, gur ... (*forms adjectives in Accadian*)	𒄘	gu, tsarapu, tsamadusa-narcabti, macaru - sa - macuri, sizbu	*purifier, chariot-yoke, cord for wares, ambrosia*
227a. ili ... ... guru ...	𒄘 𒀀	nasu, saku, makhru, guru (*from Acc.*)	*to raise, top, front, ?*
228. lakh(lakhkha)	𒄙	misu	*pure*
lakh, lukh, śun	,,	pasisu, ardu... ...	*defamer, servant*
succal, lukh	,,	succallu	*intelligence (messenger)*
nakh (*in Susian*)	,,		
229. al	𒀠	allu	name of the character
230. mis (miz), rid, lak	𒈨	idlu, karā, sangu, cirbannu	*hero, to call, chain, gift (tax)*
†cisib ...	,,	rittu	name of the character
sit (siti) ...	,,	alittu, madadu, minutu, sadhru	*genetrix, to measure, number, to write*
ak	,,	idku	*ring (?)*
†alal, †pisan	,,	pisannu, natsabu-sa-etsi	*papyrus, shaft of a tree*
231. †alal, †dibbi-sak	𒁹	natsabu-sa-kani, duppu-sadhru	*shaft of a reed, written tablet*
sak	,,	Nabū	*the god Nebo*
232. gut(gud),khar, †dapara,lē,am	𒄞	alpu, lū	*bull, herd*
†telal ...	,,	ecimmu	*bull-like demon*
233. ama ...	𒀫	rīmu	*a wild bull*

Phonetic Value (Accadian word).	Cuneiform Character.	Assyrian rendering.	Meaning.
233. cus, billudu		billudū	?
garza ...	,,	partsu	*captain (law)*
234. mascim ...		rabitsu	*an incubus*
235. sabra ...		sabru	?
236. nuzcu ...		nuscu	*Nuscu* (identified with *Nebo*)
237. sib (śiba) ...		ri'u, belu	*shepherd, lord*
238. sab (sap),‡gistar-urassa-cu ("*compound of gistar and uras*")		sabbu, gablu, saramu	name of character, *interior, to sacrifice*
239. e		kābu, bitu, kabu ...	*hollow, house, to speak*
240. duk ...		sacunu	*a building*
lut	,,	pulgu, carpatu ...	*choice, cup*
241. un		nisu	*man*
† ucu ...	,,	uku (*from Acc.*) ...	*people*
† calama ...	,,	matu	*country*
241. dan ...		dannu	*strong*
cal,†gurus ...	,,	asdhu, akru, dannu, egiru, asaridu	?, *costly, mighty*, ?, *eldest*
lab, lib, rib ...	,,	idlu	*a warrior*
† gurus ...	,,	gurusu, idlu ...	*a warrior, a hero*
zan, śim ...	,,	mātu	*country*
242. am		rīmu	*wild bull*
243. uzu		sīru	*flesh (limb, health)*
244. ne, iz (izi) ...		isatu, napakhu, izu	*fire, to dawn*, name of character
bi, pi, bil, pil, †gibil	,,	kalū	*to burn*
dhe	,,	cararu, essetu, sussu	*to revolve, new, sixty*
cum (*of Ass. origin*)	,,	camu	*to burn*
zakh ...		nāru	*daylight*

Phonetic Value (Accadian word).	Cuneiform Character.	Assyrian rendering.	Meaning.
245. gi, gibil ...		kalū, bu'idu... ...	*to burn, a spirit*
246. gil, śim ...		?, idguru	*" construction, wall, to glide"* (Lenormant), *sultriness*
247. guk		cibuśu, garru, nis-dinu	*trampling, expedition, cat* (?)
248. nir		śarru, malicu, ebilu	*king, prince, lord*
249. acar (See 68a.)		aplukhtu	*reverence*
250. ub (up), ār (ara)		cipru, tupku, garmu, enakhu	*region, zone, quarter, to decay*
251. mebulug (*of Ass. origin*)		mebulugu, sabuccu...	*choice, ?*
251a. ?		śinu...	*the moon*
252. gab, dū, takh, dukh		makharu, irtu, daku, padharu, padi, isi, dakhadu, nadhalu, naśikhu, etsibu, saninu, nadhalu, sakhatu	*front, breast, to strike, to deliver, ?, he has, to rejoice, to raise, a remover, to establish, a rival, to transfer, to destroy*
takh ...	„	labanu-libanu ...	*brickwork*
	„	radu	*descent* (or *thunderbolt*)
253. zin		tseru	*desert (against, over)*
zer (*of Ass. origin*)	„		
† rabita ...	„	iztati	*?*
254. takh ...		etsibu, uraddu ...	*to establish, to dispose*
255. sam ...		sīmu	*price*
256. zik (zig), khas		zikku, sabru, garru ...	*to break* (?), *expedition* (?)
257. uru		aru, epuru	*?, fecundity*
‡ ugudili ...	„	esgurru	*?*
258. ?		?	*?*

Phonetic Value (Accadian word).	Cuneiform Character.	Assyrian rendering.	Meaning.
259. usbar		uspa-rabu, emu ...	great quiver, quiver
uzu	„	barū...	?
260. urugal ...		gabru	opposer (hero)
261. sam... ...		?	?
262. aca		rāmu, nasu, madadu, maharu	high, to raise, to measure, to urge on
ram (Ass. value)	„		
263. ?		?	?
264. lab, rud, unu		alu	city
265. agarin ...		ummu	mother (?)
266. ?		śarru	king
267. ubigi ...		partsu or tamtsu ...	shrine (?)
268. ?		?	?
269. gaz (gaza), caś		dāku, niku, buhuz, khibu	to smite, victim, sacrifice, wanting (?)
270. lil, ubi, gud †galam, †galum		abutu, śaru, naclu, melu, alpu	charm, king, complete, fullness, bull
271. ?		?	?
272. zicura ...		irtsitu	the earth
273. taltal ...		Ea	the god Ea
274. śi, se,†sem ...		nadanu, sacaru ...	to give, to give
	„	nadu, śapanu, idu, sāmu, palaśu	to place, to sweep away, to lay, to set, to weigh (be favourable)
śi,†śunnu ...	„	sananu-sa-*, lavu-sa-*	geometrical figure, tablet of *

Phonetic Value (Accadian word).	Cuneiform Character.	Assyrian rendering.	Meaning.
275. rakh, †ukhula		rapaśu, khālu, ramacu, ukhulu	to thresh, to turn, to dwell, a calf (?)
276. śar		sadhru, muśaru, sumu	to write, an inscription, name
khir, khur ...	„	zarakhu, zamaru, dharudu, atsu-sa-etsi-u-kani	to rise, to dawn, to repel, growth of trees and grass
khir, †cesda, †essa	„	arku, raciśu, rucuśu, ciru, calū, nabu, caśu	green (leaf), to bind, bond, enclosure, all, to proclaim, to cover
†cismakh, *gū	„	samu	sky
277. ubara ...		cididu	glow (spark)
	„	cidinu, rimutu, nira-rutu	protection (law), grace, help
278. asilal ...		risātu	eldest (first)
279. bat		dūru, mitutu ...	fortress, death
280. dadhrū ...		dabibu	deviser
281. mermer ...		Rammanu	the air-god (Rimmon)
282. lū		dalakhu	to trouble
guk	„	cuccu	?
283. gā, de ...		taru, nacaru, passakhu, napalu, nakamu, ecimu, cipupi, palakhu, calalu, sabadhu, nacru-sa-amati	to return, to change, to pass over, to throw down, to punish, to strip, ?, to worship, to complete, staff (?), breaker of faith
284. cus		nākhu, nikhu, tsalamu	to rest, rest, shadow (eclipse)
śur, sur ...	„	iśśu	mighty
‡sagga-gunū ("sak with additions")	„	izzis, uzzis ...	strongly (?)
285. ra		rakhatsu, akhazu, ana, rapasu, tsabatu	to inundate, to take, to (for), to enlarge, to seize
sà ...	„	lā, lū, ina	not, then, in

Phonetic Value (Accadian word).	Cuneiform Character.	Assyrian rendering.	Meaning.
285. kal (?) ...	𒆗	cipru	*region (race)*
286. uśan ...		?	?
286a. ?	(*in Pers. Insc.*)	napalcutu	*rebel*
287. sa, gum, cū, mulu, lugur, nita		nisu, avilu	*man, man*
287a. azalak ...		azlacu	?
287b. dinik ...		sibtsu	?
287c. khara ...		izkhabbu	?
288. sis		akhu, urinnu ...	*brother*, name of the character
ur (uru) ...		natsaru, nuru ...	*to help, light*
289. da [*individualising affix in Acc.*]		racabu, nasū-sa-nisi	*to drive, top of a man*
		pidhnu	*yoke (furrow)*
290. zak (śak), zik		zaggu, amutu, ebiltu, adi, isaru, idu, itatu, pūlū, bircu, atsidu, isdu, bamatu, tsēru, emuku, asaridu, sumelu, ricśu, pādu, esrit	*truth, lordship, up to, just (straight), house, wall, cattle, knee, ?, heap, high place, supreme, deep, eldest, left hand, bond (building), frontier, shrine*
†tami ..	,,		
†zikkad ...	,,	simtu	*destiny*
291. ma,†mamū ...		sacanu, padinnu, mātu	*to dwell, plain, country*
		zacaru	*to commemorate*
292. as		arratu, ciccinu, tsibutu, khasakhu, madadu	*curse (enchantment), ?, wish, want, to measure*
†dessu ...	,,	samu, khibanu ...	*heaven, want*
293. gal, [tak *in Susian.*]		gallu, rabu	*great, great*
293a. utaccal ...		utaccilu, basmu ...	*sacrificial flame*
293b. ulad ...		dabikhu	?

Phonetic Value (Accadian word).	Cuneiform Character.	Assyrian rendering.	Meaning.
293c. kigal ...		muhirru	*ruler*
294. ?		karū	*to invoke*
295. mir, †ega ... ‡dhun-gunū ("*dhu with additions*")		agu, banu, uzzu ... śibbu, śibkhū, iltanu	*crown (halo), tiara, coronet girdle, turban* (Heb. מִסְפַּחַת), *north* (?)
296. bar (bara) ...		paraccu, basamu, udu, risku	*altar (sacrifice), balsam, aloe, nard*
sar (sara) ...	„	sāru, sarru, paracu ...	*king, prince*
297. bur, gul (?) ‡ninda-gunū ("*ninda with additions*")		isdu, būru, śalatu-sa-*, abnu	*heap,* name of the character, *?, stone*
298. bis (pis), ‡kha-gunū (" *kha with additions*")		gabbaru, palakhu, rapadu, mamluv, khuzabu, salalti, napasu	*hero (strong), to worship, ?, rain, clay (?), spoiling, to tear*
kir (cir), gar	„	cabattu	*liver*
299. gar, kar ...		abbuttu, karru ...	*?,* name of the character
300. pir		?	?
301. id		idu, ikhitu, cuśśu ...	*hand (power), one* (fem.), *throne* [the character seems originally to have denoted *a comb*], *might, ?*
		emuku, labicu ...	
a	„	karnu	*horn*
302. ?		paratsu	*to speak falsely*
303. uru, muru, †murub		gablu	*the middle (battle)*
unu	„	nasacu, niku, subtu, biru	*to pour out, libation, seat, ?*
304. de, dim ...		saku-sa-ikli, sicitu, tupuku, nas'u, śiśitu	*top of a field, surface* (?), *district, to tear up (remove),?*
śi, †śimuk, †idgal	„	nappakhu	*to dawn*
†umun	„	mummu	?
†ubil	„	sagumu	?

Phonetic Value (Accadian word).	Cuneiform Character.	Assyrian rendering.	Meaning.
305. ?		?	"hermaphrodite" (Oppert)
306. lil		lillu	sorcery (?)
307. śukh, lukh, lakh śig		tsabatu, ri'u, tallicu ... alacu, cānu, uzuzu ...	to seize, shepherd, a march to march, to establish, to fix
308. ?		pulu	cattle
309. alam, alala, biseba lani, sabaru	"	tsalamu ... ... bunnu	image image (sculpture)
310. bisebi ...		samsu	the sun
311. khilib ...		ilu	god
312. ?		belatu	lady
313. śik, śizi, ara...	"	arku, urcitu ... ... banu	green, verdure old gazelle
314. dub ... ... †balag ...	"	napatsu, egu ... balangu	to break in pieces, to surround division
315. sa ... ... †nā	"	lu, nasu ... ... pidhnu	?, to take away yoke
316. acada, burbur, uri		tilla, saki	highland (Accad), the summits
317. su, †sugab, kat		katu, idu, gimillu, emuku, ubanu	hand, hand (power), benefit, hollow, peak
317a. khul (?) ...		nigū, gamalu ...	control (?), to benefit
317b. tucundi ...		summa	thus (if)
318. curu ... (See No. 111.)		damiku	prosperous

Phonetic Value (Accadian word).	Cuneiform Character.	Assyrian rendering.	Meaning.
319. sâ		damaku	*fortunate*
†gisimmar ...	,,	gisimmaru	*trunk (of a tree)*
320. lab, lul, ruk, nar, rar, pakh, lib		śarru	*king*
320. se		ûm *or* im, ziru, ittu, amaru, magaru	*corn (grain), seed, wheat, wheat, happy*
†niga ...	,,	marū	*young*
† sana, †sananabacu	,,	irbittu	*four*
		?	*hin (a measure)*
321. bu (pu), śir, gid		śeru, sadadu, ericu, nūru, cisadu, bussusu	*long, to extend, light, bank, ?*
†sepuz ...	,,	maru, naśakhu, rabadhu, ebiru	*young, to remove, to adorn (?), to cross*
śus, guz ...	,,	napakhu, Davcina ...	*to dawn, the goddess Daukê*
322. ?		?	*?*
323. sud		ericu, rukutu ...	*to extend, distant*
śu	,,		
†ezu	,,	arū, zaraku, śulukhu, irisu, sakhalu	*?, bucket (?), pardon (?), request (?), plague (?)*
‡śir-gunū ("*śir with additions*")			
324. tsir (śir) ...		tsiru	*serpent*
mus	,,	musu	*serpent (?)*
325. uz (uts, uś), śir		uśu, tsiru	*name of the character, serpent*
326. tir (ter) ...		cisatu (kistu), dayanu,	*jungle, judge*
327. te, †dimmenna		temennu, tsabatu, cuśśu	*floor (foundation-stone), to seize, throne*
te, dikh (*of Ass. origin*)	,,	dakhu	*to face*
327*a*. mulla ...		?	*?*
327*b*. unu, ‡temenes-gunū ("*te and es with additions*")		maca *	*

Phonetic Value (Accadian word).	Cuneiform Character.	Assyrian rendering.	Meaning.
328. car		caru, ediru, ecimu, dakhu	*fortress, to arrange (fortress), to strip, to face*
329. u		belu, śaru, ubanu, śilu	*lord, king, peak, rock*
pur, bur ...	,,	esritu, suplu ...	*ten, below*
†ge	,,	mikhiltu	*battle*
†umun ...	,,	damu	*blood (offspring)*
329a. udun ...		utunu	?
330. babar ...		putstsū-sa-kan-dubba	*white surface to receive an inscription*
331. si, lim (liv, lĭ)		enu, amaru, makharu	*eye, to see, before (witness)*
†igi ...	,,	panu, igu	*presence (face), name of ch.*
(See No. 39)	,,	mātu, ecitsu ...	*country, ?*
ir (?), tim (?)	,,	alapu	*symbol of* 1000.
332. khul ...		kullulu, limuttu, khumkhum	*accursed (evil), baneful, sultry*
333. curuv ...		pakadu, damku ...	*overseer, propitious (of good omen)*
333a. ?		khāru	*to engrave*
334. seba, izcu (?)		tugultu, ardutu, libittu	*service, servitude, omen*
335. ?		?	*(astronomical) observation*
336. pam (pav, pā)		zacaru, nabu, tamatu, namru, utu	*to remember, to proclaim, remember, bright, ?*
337. ar		?	?
338. ?		nemicu	*deep wisdom*
339. va		u, naku, śarru ...	*and, to sacrifice, king*
†tsi	,,		
‡igi-dippi ("*igi and dip*")			
340. timkhir ...		Nabiuv	*the god Nebo*
341. pikh ...		?	?

Phonetic Value (Accadian word).	Cuneiform Character.	Assyrian rendering.	Meaning.
342. di,†dim ...	〈⼁〉, ⼁⼀	dēnu (dīnu), salamu, śulmu, erisu, sananu, sakabu, śararu, casadu	*to judge, to end, rest, to ask, to rival, to make speak, ?, to conquer*
śa	,,	milcu, śarar-śirri ...	*king (judge), ?*
śilim, sallim (*of Ass. origin*)	,,	śulmu, sulummu ...	*rest (completion, recompense), peace (alliance)*
342a. śagar, śagalum	〈⼁ ⼤	malicu	*a king*
343. ci (cina¸,†cicū	⼁⼀, 〈⼁⼀	itti (ittu), asru, kakkaru, mātu, irtsitu, saplu, asābu, anna, ema, subtu	*with, place, ground, country, earth, lower, a dwelling, on, about, a seat*
†cizlukh ...	,,	mascanu	*high place*
343a. utu ...	〈⼁⼀ 〈⼁⼀	citim-sa	*below it (its lower part)*
343b. cancal ...	〈⼁⼀ ⼀⼁⼁⼁	suluv, nidutu, terictu, asru, ramanu	*high, high place, high place, place, high place*
343c. siten ...	〈⼁⼀ ���	malacu	*to rule or journey (?)*
344. gurrud ...	⼁〈⼁	kharru	*?*
345. minnabi ...	〈⼁⼁⼁	sū	*like (the same, ditto, repetition)*
346. cusi... ...	〈⼁⼁⼁	?	*?*
347. sakkad ...	〈⼀⼁⼁⼀	cubsu, Nabiuv ...	*crown, the god Nebo*
348. lit, lat (lad)...	〈⼀	?	*?*
†ab	,,	arkhu	*month*
†u	,,	... ...	*... ... ...*
349. cir (kir) ...	〈⼁⼁⼁	cīru, tsurru	name of the character, *bowels*
ub	,,	ubbu	name of the character
†libis... ...	,,	labbu	*heart (interior)*
sem... ...	,,	khalkhallatu ...	*desire (?)*
350. metsi ...	〈⼁⼀⼀⼁⼁	manzu	*?*

Phonetic Value (Accadian word).	Cuneiform Character.	Assyrian rendering.	Meaning.
351. ‡sâ-gira-cu-a-igi-idu ("*within cir a and igi are placed*")		ditanu, cabtu ...	*chamois* (?), *glorious*
351a. alim ...		Bilu, śarru, Beltu, mitanu, cuśariccu	*the god Bel, king, goddess Beltis, plague,* ?
352. cis (kis) ...		[cissatu]	*multitude (abbreviation)*
353. ner		sepu...	*foot (basis)*
ne,†pisim ...	„	emuku	*deep*
†aric... ...	„	nēru, pisimmu ...	*yoke,* ?
	„	namru	*bright*
354. tidnu ...		akharru	*behind (the west)*
355. liliś		liliśu...	*barrier* (?)
356. zigarū ...		samū	*heaven*
357. sacan (?) ...		sacanu	*to appoint*
357. ‡sa-dugacu-nu-na-idu ("*within duga is placed nuna*")		'ublu, nakhagunmatu, parsu'hu, śaśu, mūnu, selibbū	*worm,* ?, *flea, moth, worm, worm*
dūgu... ... (*See No.* 414)		bircu, dābu, rikhu ...	*knee, good, odour* (or *breath*)
358. gingir ...		Istar	*the goddess Istar*
359. amar ...		buru, gannu... ...	*light* (*glory*), *enclosure*
zur (*of Ass. origin*)	„	tsūru	*splendour*
360. śigisse ...		niku, taslu, ciribu ...	*victim, prayer, offering*
361. nim, num, nū		saku, elamu, zību ...	*top, highland (Elam), wolf*
†enum (enuv)	„	samū	*heaven*
	„	nakaru - sa - semiri, garru, zumbu	*cutting by means of the diamond,* ?, *a fly*
362. zum ...		napalu	*to destroy*

Phonetic Value (Accadian word).	Cuneiform Character.	Assyrian rendering.	Meaning.
363. tum... ...		babalu, sa-elamacu...	to bring down (produce), who am high (?)
364. lam (lav) ...		lammu	name of the character
365. nū		rabatsu	to rest
366. nā		udhalu (utalu) ...	eclipse (setting)
gud ...		rabatsu, nadu, mayalu	to lie down, to settle, bed
367. ul, dū,‡udbu-guddhu		cacabu	star
		pakadu	to oversee
ru	,,	elipu - sa - etsi, śumu, surru, calulu, tac-cabu, muttacbu	ship of wood, ?, ?, ?, revolution, revolving
368. cir (kir) ...		śalkhu (?)	citadel
369. bam, ban, bav		mitpanu, kastu ...	bow, bow
370. dim,†sitimmu		cima, summa, banu, episu, basū, sama-dhu, matsū	like, thus, to form, to make, to be, ?, to find
tum (tuv)	,,	banu, kharatsu, khar-tsu	to produce, to create, ob-scurity
cim, gim (of Ass. origin)	,,	... ...	... ...
	,,	idinnu	?
371. sita		ricśu, patlulu ...	bond, mixed (?)
372. ✳ ruv, gir ...		cīrū	?
373.		aculu	eating
374. mi, vi,†gig,†cu		tsalmu, eribu ...	shade (black), sunset
ge	,,	musu	night
†cuga ...	,,		
375. śun		nardapu	pursuit (?)
gul (kul) ...	,,	abatu	to destroy
	,,	subtu, calu-sa-avili ...	seat, whole of a man

Phonetic Value (Accadian word).	Cuneiform Character.	Assyrian rendering.	Meaning.
376. dugud ... cab (*Ass. value*)	〈≡≡〉, 〈≡≡- "	cabdu, miktu ...	*heavy (much, honor),* ?
377. gig ...	〈≡≡⟩⟨	martsu, śimmu, cibtu	*sick, plague, affliction*
378. din (tin) ... gal	⟨⟨, ⟨ "	baladhu ... ... bitu	*life (family)* *house*
379. ugun ...	〈⊢⟩⟨	akhzētu, Naná ...	?, *the goddess Nana*
380. mukh ...	〈⊢⊢	mukhkhu, eli, banu, alidu	*over, over, to create, to beget*
381. caccul ...	〈⊢⟨≡≡, 〈⊢⟨≡	kakkullu, namzitu ...	?, ?
382. man, in, nis † buśur ... śar (*Ass. value*)	〈〈 " "	śaru ... ... samsu, esrā	*king* *the sun, twenty*
383. cus (cusu) ...	〈〈≡	pulu...	*sunset*
384. es ... ... † esseb ... śin (*Ass. value*)	〈〈〈 " "	bitu ... ... salasā, Śinu ...	*house* *thirty, the Moon*
385. sanabi ...	⟨〈〈	irbahā	*forty*
386. usu, sa ...	〈 ⊣⟩	erib-samsi	*sunset*
387. nigin ...	〈 ⊣⟩ ⊨⟩⟩⟩	cummu, iśpu ...	*the interior of the earth, evening*
388. lagar ...	〈⟨⟨⟨	lagaru	?
389. cizlukh (?) ...	〈⟨⊨⟩	mascanu	*high*
390. tul (dhul) ...	〈≡⟩, 〈≡⟩	tilu, ridu-sa-riduti, sadu	*mound, harem, hill*
dul	"	catanu	*to conceal*
mul... ...	"	mulu	?
390a. ?	〈≡⟩ ⊨⟩	subū, elu	*made to come, to ascend*

4

Phonetic Value (Accadian word).	Cuneiform Character.	Assyrian rendering.	Meaning.
391. cū, ri ...		ellu, caśpu	high (noble, precious), silver (money)
391a. babbar, cubabbar ... azak (?) ...		caśpu, tsarpu ...	silver, silver
391b. guski ...		khuŕatsu	gold
392. mun ...		idlū	a hero
393. dun... ... sul	”	idlu, dannu ... ... śulum	hero, strong ?
394. eśa, śa ...		khamesserit, Istar, imnu	fifteen, the goddess Istar, right hand
395. pad (pat), kur (?) ... suk	”	śimtu, sipartu ... curastu	settlement, bill (account) baggage
396. gam (gū) ... lus, gur ...		iśacu, lanu, kanduppi, musacnis, cubuśu, kabu gamasu	to pour (?), a dwelling, a papyrus-scroll, subduer, a trampling, to speak to cajole
397. *		Sign of a division	between words or sentences
398. *		do.; also a	contracted form of the number 9
399. cur (kur) ... mat (mad) ... lat (lad), nat (nad), sat (sad) †ra'er ...	” ” ”	curu, sadu, elu, garu, nacaru, napakhu mātu, casadu ... mātu, sadu	land, mountain (the east), high, foreign, hostile, to dawn country, to conquer (acquire) country, mountain
400. ana		... ...	to root up
401. lis, dil (dul)		iddu * *	?

Phonetic Value (Accadian word.)	Cuneiform Character.	Assyrian rendering.	Meaning.
402. ud (utu, ut), par, khiś		samsu, yumu, namaru, enu, nahru-sa-yumi, urru, pitsu, atsu	sun, day, to see, eye, dawning of day, light, white, to rise
lakh... ...	,,	samsu, śarru, ellu ...	sun, king, high
zal (śal), tam	,,	samsu	the sun
† sam (,u) ...	,,	yumu, immu, samsu	the day, the day, the sun
zab,†erim ...	,,	tsābu, bibu	soldier (host), clear
† babar ...	,,	tsit-samsi, namaru ...	sunrise, to see
		tihamtu	the deep
402a. e		atsu, makhkhu, padu	to rise (issue), mighty, sceptre
402b. ukh (ukhu) (see 405)		cusu, ruhtu...	?, poison (?)
402c. zabar ...		śiparru, cemas ...	copper (bronze), ditto
403. bir		nuru, namaru ...	light, to see
† erim, lakh ...	,,	tsabbu	soldier (host)
zab, śab (Ass. values)			
403a. nunuz ...		pilu	choice
404. ?		niraru	helper
405. ukh... ...		ruhtu	poison (philtre)
406. pi		uznu	ear
ā, tal, pi, me (Ass. value)	,,	me, giltanu	water, drop
407. 'ā, āh ...		giltanu	drop of water
408. sā, lib,†śini ...		labbu, pukhru ...	heart (middle, within), assembly
408a. śini ...		kunkut [or kuntar] ...	?
409. pis		eru, aladu	pregnant, begetting
410. bir		saradhu	to cut open
411. nanam ...		cinu	established (firm)

4*

Phonetic Value (Accadian word).	Cuneiform Character.	Assyrian rendering.	Meaning.
412. gudu ...	◁𝇇𝇈𝇈	?	*to set (end)*
413. zib (śib, tsib)	𝅘	zibbu	?
414. khi,†khig ...	◁ (*also written* ◁)	dhābu, cissatu, esiru	*good, multitude, propitious (holy)*
dhi, khā ...	„	cissatu-sa-same, bircu	*legions of heaven, a knee*
†id, sar (śarrab), śib (zib), dhum	„	... ...	*a measure*
dar, dhar ...	„	pallilu, Assuru ...	*to mingle, the god Assur*
sar,†dūgu (*See No.* 357)	„	cissatu, mādu, rabu, bukhudu, sutabū, dussu, nukhsu, pumalu, nakhasu-sa-nukhsi, rikhu, sutemū	*multitude, much, great, great, ?, ?, prosperity, powerful, prosperer of prosperity, sweet odour, ?*
415. im, †ni ...	◁𝇈	rukhu, rikhu, ramanu, palakhu, rarubatu	*wind (air, tempest, cardinal point), breath, self, to worship, fear*
sar	„	sāru, samu	*brightness (sky), heaven*
†mir,†muru ...	„	nahdu, irbu, Rammanu	*bright, rain, the Air-god*
im, †ni ...	„	pulukhtu, emuku, zumru, au	*fear, deep, body (person), wind*
†imi	„	samu, irtsitu, akhu, didu, sāru, zunnu, duppu	*sky, earth, brother (?), ?, wind, rain, tablet (?)*
415a. latakh ...	◁𝇈 𝇊	uduntu-sa-rukhi ...	*quantity of wind*
416. kam (cam), kham, du	◁𝇏	... ...	denotes ordinal numbers
416a. esses ...	◁𝇏 𝇎𝇎𝇎	?	?
417. ah (h, hi) ...	◁𝇒𝇓, ◁𝇒 (*in Persian inscriptions*)	'umunu	*small worm*

Phonetic Value (Accadian word).	Cuneiform Character.	Assyrian rendering.	Meaning.
418. akh, ikh, ukh, (ukhu)		uplu, kalmatu, pursu'u, umunu	*worm, vermin, flea, small worm*
	„	rukhuku	*distant*
†lammubi ...	„	nāpu	*worm*
419. bir		sapikhu	*a destroyer*
420. khar ... mur, ur, cin, kham		semiru, esiru ... cirbu, khasu, zumru, libbi, cima	*diamond, bracelet* *centre, liver, body, heart, ?*
	„		
420a. urus (= *the god Bel in Cassite*)		tirtu, tirtu-sa-khasē ...	*body (form), the intestines*
421. khus (khuś) rus		khussu ... ... russu	*beaten out (small gazelle)* *young gazelle, blue cloth*
	„		
422. śukh, †śukhar		cimmatu	*family (household)*
423. zun		mahdutu	*many*
424. ?		belatu	*lady*
425. ?		rabu, dannu ...	*great, strong*
426. zicara ...		samu	*the sky*
427. dis (tis), gi ... ana (*Ass. value*)		ana, śarru, estinu ...	*to, king, one*
	„		
428. lal		malu, madhu, sapacu, sakalu, ubburu-sa-amati, khizu, sapalu, etsilu, śaradu-sa-cipratu, śanaku, cima, tartsu, callu, ensu, anunnaci	*to fill, weak, to pour out, to weigh (pay), transgression of oath, ?, under (below), to join, terror of heaven (name of a bird), chain, like, facing (in the time of), to restrain, sick, spirits of earth*
nas, lū ...	„	sakalu, tsabatu, tsimdu, nīru, aniru, khatsapu	*to weigh, to seize, yoke, yoke, yoke, to be thick*
429. lal, ū ...		sukalulu	*to equal (reach)*

Phonetic Value (Accadian word).	Cuneiform Character.	Assyrian rendering.	Meaning.
430. usar... ...		settu	*bank*
431. ucu		labnu	*brick*
432. nanga ...		nagu (*of Acc. origin*)	*a district*
433. lalu		libbātu	*brickwork*
434. me (eme) ...		kulu, kālu, tamtsu, zicaru, takhatsu, dūtu, meh, samu	*voice, to call, mass, memorial, battle, ?, 100, sky, sign of the plural*
†isip, sib (sip) (*of Ass. origin*)	,,	ramcu	*a resting-place*
435. mes (mis) ...		mahdutu, libbu ...	*many, heart, sign of the plural*
436. kas, men, mema minnabi ...	,,	sinu, sanu	*two, repetition (ditto)*
437. 'a (*forms participles in Acc.*)	(*also written*)	me, abu, 'ablu ...	*water, father, son*
pur	,,	nahru	*river*
† dur	,,	labacu	*?*
†it	,,	nāku	*pure (sacrifice)*
†ga, e ...	,,	rakipu	*?*
437a. eba ...		melu	*flood*
437b. ara... ...		milcu	*a going*
437c. ir		dimtu, calū naccalu, unninnu	*a tear, complete vessel, prayer*
437d. aria, hid ...		nahru	*river*
438. ai		abu	*father*
439. ?		iddu...	*bitumen*
440. kurnun ...		Tasmitu	*the goddess Tasmit (wife of Nebo)*
441. za (tsa) ...		arbu, ci, atta ...	*four, thee, thou*

Phonetic Value (Accadian word).	Cuneiform Character.	Assyrian rendering.	Meaning.
441a. uknu ...	𒊏	ibbu	*white*
442. kha	𒄩	nunu, ranu, simru, nabu, khalaku	*fish, ?, ?, to proclaim, to divide (destroy)*
'a, cua ...	,,	Cū'a	*Merodach's oracle*
443. gug (guk) ...	𒄖	śamtu	*blue*
444. zakh ...	𒍠	?	*?*
444. ner ...	𒐕	nēr	*measure* or *space of six hundred*
445. dar, ara ...	𒐖	?	80
446. essa, mus ...	𒐈	salsatu	*three*
446a. gar or sā ...	𒐉	ribu	*a fathom*
446b. gi (?) ...	𒐐	kanu	*a cane (measure)*
447. †sana, sa ... †irba (*Ass. value*)	𒐞 ,,	irbu, ribu, nitu (nindu)	*four, a quarter,* name of the character
gar	,,	episu, sacanu, saracu, girū, naśakhu-satirti, rakhatsu, zaltu, nūru, khamdhu, gamalu, maśakhu, garru, sēmu, zaltu, acalu, cumuru, sucunnu, eristu	*to make (do), to dwell, to furnish, hostile, removal of body, to inundate, granary, light, speedy, to benefit, removal, food, obedient, ?, food, ?, fortress, bride (?)*
sā	,,	?, mala, nasu ...	*a measure* (a quart), *as many as, to lift up*
448. śa, †para ...	𒐊	khamsa	*five*
ya, i ...	,,	nahdu	*glorious*
449. as	𒐋	sissu	*six*
450. sisna ...	𒐌	śibu	*seven*
451. ?	𒐍 , 𒐏, 𒑁	tisu	*nine*

Phonetic Value (Acca-dian word).	Cuneiform Character.	Assyrian rendering.	Meaning.
452. nin		allatu	*wife*
453. kap, gubbu...		sumelu	*the left hand*
454. esseb ...		sarru	*king*
455. duk, tuc (tug) dū		tucu, isu, akhazu, si-mū, zarakhu, tsa-maru	*to have, to have, to possess, to place, to rise, to rise* (of stars)
456. ur		khamamu, etsidu, na-raru, aruru, khazu	*heat* (*celestial sphere*), *side* (*of the world*), *to burn, burnt,* ?
457. sussana ...		sussanu	*one-third*
457a. gigim ...		ecimmu	*demon*
458. sanibi ...		sīnibu	*two-thirds* (*forty*)
459. utuk ...		uduccu	*spirit*
460. kiguśili, parap		parapu	*five-sixths*
461. mascim ...		mascimmu	*a demon*
462. cu		usibu, subtu, marcaśu, ina, ana, rubū, akru, tucultu	*to sit down, seat, bondage, in, to, prince, precious, service*
‡ip-utu-gula-cu ("*ip with great ut*")	„		
dur, pī, tul...	„	tucultu, nukhu, zacaru	*service, rest, to record*
us	„	dhemu	*law*
zi	„	cemu	*clothes*
tū	„	nadu, tsubatu ...	*to place, clothes*
se	„	tucullu	*purple robe*
tus,(dus),khun, †seba,†mugu	„		
	„	nasu-sa-eni, muśaru, dū, tsillu, mulū, succu, subat-sa-apśi	*raising of the eyes, inscription,* ?, *side, ascent* (?), *booth, seat of the underworld*

Phonetic Value (Accadian word).	Cuneiform Character.	Assyrian rendering.	Meaning.
463. gil, khap (khab), gur (gu), cir, (kir, gir), rim, †girim, gar, zam, mik, †lagab (*See No.* 481)	⟡	lagabu	?
	„	racaśu, pukhkhuru, gararu-sa-nisi, śecuru, dubutu, bahalu, bihisu	*to bind, gathering, tumult of men, enclosing, ?, tumult, ?*
463a. puda (gidda)	⟡ 𒌋	aricu, ruku	*long, distant*
464. zar (tsar, śar)	𒌋	?	?
465. umuna ...	𒌋	alapu	*a thousand* "*festival*" (Lenormant)
466. zarip ...	𒌋	?	?
467. uh, ua ...	𒌋	rubtsu, cabasu, pikannu	*flock, sheep*
468. ?	𒌋	taccabu	*revolution*
469. suk ... ... †umun ...	𒌋 „	tsutsu ... ... khammu	*aquatic plant (plant, marsh)* *heat (zone)*
470. pu ... ... pur (*See No.* 223)	⟨, ⟨ „	tsutsu ... ... pūru, muspalu ...	*pool (marsh)* *pool (?), low ground*
471. bul	𒌋	mamma	*somebody*
472. ?	𒌋	?	*a cornfield (?)*
473. ?	𒌋	?	?
474. cu (?) *or* sāgar (?)	𒌋	khusukhkhu ...	*famine*

Phonetic Value (Accadian word).	Cuneiform Character.	Assyrian rendering.	Meaning.
475. sū		zirku	*a bucket*
476. gur		apśu...	*running water*
‡zicum ...	,,	samū	*heaven*
477. ?		?	?
478. ?		iddu (*see No.* 439) ...	*bitumen*
479. ?		narcabtu	*chariot*
480. ?		pagru	*corpse*
481. nigin ...	(*See No.* 463)	napkharu, pakharu, śakharu, nagarruru, tsai'idu, tsadu-salavē, pasaru, epusu, racaśu	*collection, to collect, to surround, tumultuous assembly, hunter, hunter of the neighbourhood, to enclose, to make, to bind*
‡cili			
‡ilammi ...	,,		
481*a*. ‡cilidagal ...		?	*library*
482. ?		*	*such an one (so and so)*
483. ip (ib, ibbi)...		banu, ligittu, tupuktu	*to create, log* (measure), *region*
dar	,,	nibittu, gisru ...	*name, strong*
‡darum ...	,,	izkhu	?
‡uras... ...	,,	sa-issik-icribi, baru, ramcu, urasu, acmu, ligittu, nibittu	*who hears prayers, ?, a rest, ?, ?, log, name*
484. lu		tsini, cirru	*flocks, sheep*
dib (dip) ...	,,	dibbu, lavu, etiku, tsabatu, titsbatu, tamkhu	*tablet, tablet, to cross, to seize, spoil, hold*
‡udu,‡dū ...	,,	immiru, dassu ...	*lamb, gazelle*
‡tu,‡sib (sip) ...	,,		
‡guccal ...	,,	guccallu	*sheep*
	,,	cavu, bahu, garru ...	*to burn* (?), *chaos, food*

Phonetic Value (Acca-dian word).	Cuneiform Character.	Assyrian rendering.	Meaning.
485. ki, kin (cin) gur	𒆠, 𒆠, 𒆠	turtu, sipru, pāru, si-tehu, senihu, amaru	*dove (?), writing (explanation), ?, ?, to be prostrate, messenger*
486. sak, sik ...	𒆳	saradu	*paint*
śik, ukh ...	„	supātu, sipatu, lubustu	*cloth, stuff, clothing*
mut (?) ...	„		
487. ?	𒆳, 𒆳		*plank*
487a. ?	𒆳 𒌋	tsimru	*wool*
488. sis	𒆳 𒆠	pasāsu	*to serve (?)*
busus (*Ass. value*)	„	damamu	*to perish*
489. ?	𒆳	tur-sipri	*librarian (scribe)*
490. dar (dara) ...	𒆳	dahmu	*obscure (?)*
491. munsub ...	𒆳	khirtŭ	*?*
492. gur	𒆳	carū	*?*
493. erin	𒆳	erinu	*cedar (?)*
494. lig (lik) ...	𒌨	calbu, pultu, baltu, uru	*dog, ?, ?, lion*
tas (das) ...	„	nacaru	*enemy*
lis	„		
ur (*Ass. value*)	„	nesu, kardu ...	*lion, hero*
495. dhu (dhun)	𒃲	cibu, alacu	*mass (body, weight), to go*
al	„	pāsu, apasu, sundu, rucdu	*?, ?, ?, ?*
496. śal, rak (racci)	𒊬, 𒊬	śinnistu *or* nestu, uru	*a woman, a city*
kal (gal), †mu-rub	„	uru	*a city*
mak, muk ...	„	muccu	*a building*
496a. murub ...	𒊬	uru	*a city*
496b. murub ... emes, uśukh	𒊬	pū, uśukhu	*mouth, ?*

Phonetic Value (Accadian word).	Cuneiform Character.	Assyrian rendering.	Meaning.
497. gar		nan * *	?
498. nin, ni, mak...		beltu, rubatu, mimma	*lady, princess, anyone*
499. dam (dav) ...		assatu, allatu, [mutu]	*woman, wife, [husband]*
500. gu		kā, īlu-sa-napkhari, mātu, pānu	*?, god of the world, land, face*
501. ?		amtu	*handmaiden*
502. tsu, tsum, rak, ri, khal (khil)		?	?
503. nik (nig) ...		?	?
504. i		?	?
505. el (il) ... (*See No.* 211)		śimiccu, ellu, bibu ... teliltu	*?, holy, pure* *hymn*
506. lum, khum ... sum (?) ...		unnubu	?
507. mun, mur, †ucu		labinu, libittu, malgu, Śivannu	*brick, brickwork, brick, the month Sivan*
508. ?		ussusu	*foundation*
509. su, † mastenu		baru, eribu, nikhappu, lēmu, śakhpu, asaru, śikhu, caramu, adaru, khīsu, cissatu	*?, to set, ?, ?, overthrow, a place (?), plague, a vineyard (?), darkness (?), ?, multitude*
†essā ...	,,	sepu...	*a foot*
su	,,	mastenu	name of the character
†dhim,†sumastin	,,	essutu (sanitu) ...	*change (time)*
	,,		
510. śik (sik, sig)		siktu, matsu, mātu, ensu, nadkhu, śakhpu	*?, to find (?), country, sick, fragment, overthrow*
510a. ?		?	"*a sixtieth*" (Oppert)

Phonetic Value (Accadian word).	Cuneiform Character.	Assyrian rendering.	Meaning.
511. pis		khumtsiru	?
cis	,,	peśu...	?
* mis ...	,,	citstu	*jungle*
512. ?		pulukhtu	*fear (worship)*
513. gibil ...		kilutu	*a burning*
cibir ...	,,	sarapu, makiddu ...	*to burn, a burning*
514. en		siptu	*incantation*
515. isi, śulsa, sukhul		parratu	*cow*
sukhub ...	,,	śūppatu	?
516. sutul, sudun		nīru	*yoke*
517. ?		isatu...	*fire*
518. khul ...		khidutu	*joy*
ucus ...	,,	cissu, padu	*multitude, ?*
bibra ...	,,	bibru, nigu	name of character, *authority*
519. dhul ...		?	?
520. śik		?	?
521. sikka, muna		atudu	*he-goat*
522. ?		?	*a thousandth*

N.B.—A Star (*) signifies that one or more characters have been lost by a fracture of the tablet. An Obelus (†) denotes an Accadian word which is not used as a phonetic value.

A Double Obelus (‡) marks the Accadian names of characters, the translation of which is given in parentheses.

The following is a list of the characters which express the open or simple syllables of the Assyrian alphabet. The beginner is advised to commit it to memory before advancing further in the study of the language. The letters of the Hebrew alphabet are added in order to explain the transliteration adopted for Assyrian sounds.

א, *a, à, ha* 𒀀

ב, *b.*
פ, *p.*
 ab, ib, ub.
 ba, bi, bu, be.
 pa, pi, *or* pu.

ג, *g.*
ך, *c.*
ק, *k.*
 ag, ig, ug.
 ga, gi, gu, ge.
 ca, ci, cu.
 ka, ki, ku.

ד, *d.*
ט, *dh.*
ת, *t.*
 ad, id, ud.
 da, di, du, de.
 dha, *or* dhi, dhu, dhe.
 ta, ti, tu, te.

ה, *h.* ah, hi, h, uh.

ו, *u, v.* hu, ù, u, va, u. *See also* m.

ז, *z.*
ס, *ś.*
צ, *ts.*
 az, iz, uz.
 za, zi, zu.
 śa, śi, śu.
 tsa, tsi, tsu.

ח, *kh.* akh, ikh *and* ukh, ukh; kha, khi, khu.

י, *i.* i, 'i.

ל, *l.* al, il, ul, el; la, li, *or* lu.

▢, *m*, also *v*. [cuneiform] {am, av, } [cuneiform] {im, iv, } [cuneiform] {um; uv; } | [cuneiform] *or* [cuneiform] {ma, va, } [cuneiform] {mi, vi, } [cuneiform] {nu, vu, } [cuneiform] {me. ve. }

ן, *n*. [cuneiform] an, [cuneiform] *or* [cuneiform] in, | [cuneiform] na, [cuneiform] ni, [cuneiform] nu, [cuneiform] ne. [cuneiform] un, [cuneiform] en.

ע, *e*. [cuneiform].

ר, *r*. [cuneiform] ar, [cuneiform] ir, [cuneiform] *or* | [cuneiform] ra, [cuneiform] ri, [cuneiform] *or* [cuneiform] ru. [cuneiform] ur.

ש, *s*. [cuneiform] *or* [cuneiform] as, [cuneiform] is, [cuneiform] us, | [cuneiform] *or* [cuneiform] sa, [cuneiform] si, [cuneiform] *or* [cuneiform] su, [cuneiform] es. [cuneiform] *or* [cuneiform] se.

Diphthongs :— [cuneiform] [cuneiform] ai (*aya*), [cuneiform] ya (*ia*).

An ideograph is often indicated by a *phonetic complement* which gives the first or last syllable of the Assyrian word which is to be read. Thus [cuneiform] is to be rendered by some part (according to the context) of the aorist *acsud* " I acquired."

Three main rules to be observed in selecting the value of a character are (1) that that power is to be chosen, the first or last consonant of which is the same as the consonant which ends the preceding syllable or begins the next; (2) that no Assyrian word, as a general rule, ought to contain more than three radical letters ; and (3) that values consisting only of a consonant and a vowel are to be preferred to those in which the vowel is enclosed between two consonants.

An open syllable (that is, one which begins with a vowel) only exceptionally follows a character which terminates in a consonant ; and all words end with the line. Determinative Prefixes (D.P.) are a great assistance to the reader. These are unpronounced ideographs which are always set before certain classes of persons and objects ; so that their presence enables us to tell with certainty the nature of the following word. There are also Determinative Affixes (D.A.) which serve the same purpose.

The determinative prefixes and affixes are as follows:

PREFIXES:—

('ilu)	denotes	a god or goddess.
⟨ or ⟩	„	a man.
	„	a woman.
(âlu)	„	a city or town.
(matu)	„	a country.
(nahru)	„	a river.
or (bîtu)	„	a house.
(rukhu)	„	wind, or point of the compass.
(tulu)	„	a mound.
(abnu)	„	a stone.
(illu)	„	a metal.
(etsu)	„	tree or wood.

PREFIXES:—

(kanu)	denotes	grass, reeds, &c.
('imiru)	„	animal.
(itstsuru)	„	a bird.
	„	an insect.
	„	an official or class of persons.
(bilu)	„	a ruler.
(seru)	„	a limb or body.
or (arkhu)	„	a month.
(lubustu)	„	clothing.
(cacabu) or	„	a star.
(tsini)	„	small cattle.

(sakhu) denotes a ravenous beast.

AFFIXES:—

	denotes	the plural.
	„	the dual.
	„	an ordinal number.

AFFIXES:—

(irtsitu)	denotes	a place.
(itstsuru)	„	a bird.

N.B.—It should be borne in mind that a double consonant is frequently written as though it were single; e.g., *yusacin* ( ) instead of *yusaccin* ( ).

THE NOUNS.

Nouns substantive and adjective do not differ in form in Assyrian.

The adjective always follows its substantive, and has neither comparative nor superlative.

Nouns are of two genders, masculine and feminine, and abstract nouns take the feminine form. Many words are both masculine and feminine, and may take the terminations of both genders.

There are two numbers, singular and plural; and a dual is found in the case of those nouns which denote doubles, like "the eyes." Adjectives as well as substantives admit the dual form.

There are three cases, the nominative, ending in *-u;* the genitive, ending in *-i;* and the accusative, ending in *-a ;* but great laxity prevails in the use of these forms.

The case-terminations have a final *m* (or *v*), termed the *mimmation.* This was usually dropped in the later Assyrian inscriptions, though the Babylonian dialect preserved it to the last.

When one substantive governs another, the governing noun loses the case-endings (and mimmation), and the governed noun which immediately follows commonly assumes the termination of the genitive. Thus *bil* is "lord," but *bil nuri,* "lord of light."

The feminine singular changes the *u* of the nominative masculine into *-ūtu, -ătu,* and *-ĭtu* (or *ĕtu*). The last two forms (*ătu* and *ĭtu*) might elide the vowel, unless the root is a "surd" one, like *sar,* when the final letter is doubled, producing *sarrătu,* "queen." In the plural the feminine ending became *-ātu* and *-ītu* or *-ētu.*

The oldest form of the plural masculine was in *-ānu,* which was originally used for both genders. We also find traces of a reduplicated plural, like *māmi,* "waters," and of a plural in *-ūnu,* like *dilūnu,* "buckets." Another form of the plural masculine was in *-ūtu* (carefully to be distinguished from the feminine singular in *-ūtu*). This is the form of the masculine plural adopted by all adjectives. The most common termination of the masculine plural was in *-e* or *-i.* These plurals are in many cases indistinguishable from the genitive case of the singular. The ending of the dual was *ā.*

There is a curious plural in *-tan,* which combines the feminine and masculine terminations. It expresses a *collection* of anything, e.g., *e-bir-tā-an,* "a ford."

PARADIGMS OF NOUNS.

	The Characters to be transliterated by the Student.		*The Characters to be added by the Student.*	
Masculines :—				
Sing. Nom. ...	(na - ci - ru)	*an enemy*	mu-śa-ru (*Nos.* 23, 116, 22).	*an inscription*
„ Gen. ...		...	mu-śa-ri	...
„ Acc. ...		...	mu-śa-ra	...
Plural		...	mu-śa-rē *or* mu-śa-ri	...
Sing. Construct. state		...	mu-śar	...
Sing. Nom. ...	(na - akh - lu)	*a brook*	śar-ru (*Nos.* 193, 22)	*a king*
„ Gen. ...		...	śar-ri	...
„ Acc. ...		...	śar-ra	...
Plural		...	śar-ri	...
Sing. Construct. state		...	śar	...
Sing. Nom. ...	(zic - ru)	*record*	nac-lu (*Nos.* 57, 484)	*complete*
„ Gen. ...		...	nac-li	...
„ Acc. ...		...	nac-la	...
Plural Nom. ...		...	nac-lu-tu	...
„ Gen. ...		...	nac-lu-ti	...
„ Acc. ...		...	nac-lu-ta	...

The Characters to be transliterated by the Student.			*The Characters to be added by the Student.*	
Masculines :—				
Construct. Sing.	𒀭𒀭	record	na-cal	complete
Construct. Pl....	𒀭𒀭	...	nac-lu ut...	...
Sing. Nom. ...	𒄩𒋢	fortress	khar-su	a forest
„ Gen. ...	𒄩𒋛	...	khar-si	...
„ Acc. ...	𒄩𒊝	...	khar-sa	...
Plural Nom. ...	𒄩 [or 𒄩]	...	khar-sā-nu [or khar-sa-a-nu]	...
„ Gen. ...	𒄩	...	khar-sā-ni	...
„ Acc. ...	𒄩	...	khar-sā-na	...
Construct. Sing.	𒄩	...	kha-ra-as...	...
Construct. Pl....	𒄩	...	khar-sā-an	...
Feminines :—				
Sing. Nom. ...	𒀭𒀭	a lady	'i-lā-tu	goddess
„ Gen. ...	𒀭𒀭	...	'i-lā-ti	...
„ Acc. ...	𒀭𒀭	...	'l-lā-ta	...
Plural Nom. ...	𒀭𒀭 [or 𒀭]	...	'i-lā-a tu [or 'i-lā-tu]	...
„ Gen. ...	𒀭𒀭 [or 𒀭]	...	'i-la-a-ti [or 'i-la-a-te]	...
„ Acc. ...	𒀭𒀭	...	'i-la-a-ta	...

	The Characters to be transliterated by the Student.		The Characters to be added by the Student.	
Feminines :—				
Construct. Sing.	𒊩𒌆	a lady	'l-lăt...	goddess
Construct. Pl.	𒊩𒄿𒁹𒄿	...	'i-la-a-at	...
Sing. Nom. ...	𒊩𒌅	a lady	'il-tu	goddess
„ Gen. ...	𒊩𒋾	...	'il-ti...	...
„ Acc. ...	𒊩�	...	'il-ta	...
Plural	as before	...	as before	...
Sing. Nom. ...	𒊩𒅆𒌅	...	'i-lĭ-tu	...
„ Gen. ...	𒊩𒅆𒋾	...	'i-lĭ-ti	...
„ Acc. ...	𒊩𒅆�	...	'i-lĭ-ta	...
Plural Nom. ...	𒊩𒅆𒂊𒌅	...	'i-li-e-tu ['ilētu] ...	...
„ Gen. ...	𒊩𒅆𒂊𒋾 [or 𒋼]	...	'i-li-e-ti [or 'i-li-e-te]	...
„ Acc. ...	𒊩𒅆𒂊𒘪	...	'i-li-e-ta	...
Construct. Sing.	𒊩𒌆	...	'i-lĭt	...
Construct. Pl....	𒊩𒌆	...	'i-lĭt...	...
Another Plural Noun	𒊩𒅆𒇷𒌅	a lady	'i-li-i-tu	goddess
	or 𒊩𒅆𒌅	...	or 'i-lĭ-tu	...
	&c., &c.		&c., &c.	

The Characters to be transliterated by the Student.			The Characters to be added by the Student.	
Feminines :—				
Sing. Nom. ...	𒌷𒀀	tongue	'um-mu...	mother
„ Gen. ...	𒌷𒀀	...	'um-mi	...
„ Acc. ...	𒌷𒀀	...	'um-ma...	...
Plural Nom. ...	𒌷𒀀	...	'um-ma-a-tu ['ummātu]	...
„ Gen. ...	𒌷𒀀	...	'um-ma-a-ti	...
„ Acc. ...	𒌷𒀀	...	'um-ma-a-ta	...
Construct. Sing.	𒌷𒀀	...	'um	...
Construct. Pl....	𒌷𒀀	...	'um-ma-a-at	...
Dual :—				
(Nom., Gen., Acc.)	𒌷𒀀	the two hands	'uz-na-a ('uznā)	the two ears
	or 𒌷		se-pa-a (sepa)	the two feet

Nouns to be written in Assyrian characters, and declined :—

Plural.

cu-du-du (*Nos.* 462, 212, 212)	*carbuncle*	(cu-du-de) (*Nos.* 462, 212, 342)
da-rum-mu (289, 11, 23) ...	*a dwelling*	(da-rum-mi *and* da-rum-me) (289, 11, 374 *or* 434)
ga-ru (227, 22)	*enemy*	(gari *and* ga-ri-e) (227, 83)
di-ku (342, 209)	*soldier*	(di-ku-tu) (342, 209, 60)
ci-su-du (343, 317, 212) ...	*captive*	(ci-su-du-tu) (343, 317, 212, 60)
dan-nu (241, 24)	*strong*	(dan-nu-tu) (241, 24, 60)
dup-pu (174, 321)	*tablet*	(dup-pa-a-nu) (174, 222, 437, 24)
e-mu-ku (239, 23, 209) ...	*deep power*	(e-mu-ka-a-nu) (239, 23, 20, 437, 24)
ri-su	*head*	(ri-sa-a-nu)
ci-sid-tu	*spoils*	(ci-si-da-a-tu)
i-să-tu	*fire*	('i-sa-a-tu)
pul-khă-tu *or* pu-lukh-tu ...	*fear*	(pul-kha-a-tu)
cimmă-tu *or* cim-tu	*family*	(cim-ma-a-tu)
e-li-nĭ-tu	*high*	(e-li-nē-tu)
makh-ri-tu *or* ma-khir-tu ...	*former*	(makh-ra-a-tu)
gar-ru	*expedition*	(gar-rĭ-tu *or* gar-ri-i-tu)
ag-gul-lu	*wagon*	(ag-gul-la-a-tu)
ap-pa-ru	*a marsh*	(ap-pa-ra-a-te)
ba-bu	*a gate*	(ba-ba-a-tu)

THE NUMERALS.

The cardinals have two forms, masculine and feminine; but from 3 to 10 the feminine form is used for the masculine, and the masculine form for the feminine.

When the numerals are expressed in symbols ⟨ signifies "one," ⟨⟨ "two," and so on. ⟨ stands for 10, ⟨⟨ for 11, ⟨⟨ for 20, &c. ⟨⟩ is 100, and ⟨⟨⟩ (= 10 × 100) is 1000.

The ordinals are denoted by adding ⟨⟩ to the cardinal; thus ⟨ ⟨⟩ is "first."

Sixty was the mathematical unit: the single wedge (⟨) accordingly stands for the *soss*, or *sixty*, as well as for *one*. In fractions it is the understood denominator; thus, ⟨⟨⟨ ⟨⟨⟨ (3.30) is $3 \frac{30}{60}$, *i.e.* $3\frac{1}{2}$.

TABLE OF CARDINAL AND ORDINAL NUMBERS.

			Masculine.	*Feminine.*		
1	=	⟨ (*or* ►)	a-kha-du, e-du ... es-tin, eš-ta-a-nu ...	i-khi-it ... ... ikh-tu	*First*	= makh-ru, ris-ta-a-nu
2	=	⟨⟨	sa-ni-e, sa-nu-'u, si-nu-'u	sa-ne-tu	*Second*	= san-nu (*fem.* sa-nu-tu)
3	=	⟨⟨⟨	sal-sa-tu	sal-su	*Third*	= sal-sa-ai (*fem.* sa-li-is-tu)
4	=	⟨⟨⟨⟨	ir-bit-tu, ri-ba-a-tu ...	ar-ba-'i, ir-ba'i ...	*Fourth*	= ri-bu
5	=	⟨⟨⟨⟨⟨	kha-mis-tu, kha-mil-tu	kham-sa, kha-an-si ...	*Fifth*	= kha-an-su
6	=	⟨⟨⟨⟨⟨⟨	si-sa-tu	sis-sa, sis-si ...	*Sixth*	= [? sis-su]
7	=	⟨⟨⟨⟨⟨⟨⟨	si-bit-tu, śi-bi-tu ...	śi-ba	*Seventh*	= śi-bu-'u, śa-bi-tu
8	=	⟨⟨⟨⟨⟨⟨⟨⟨	[sam-na-tu] ...	sam-na	*Eighth*	= [? śu-ma-nu]
9	=	⟨⟨⟨⟨⟨⟨⟨⟨⟨	[ti-sit-tu]	[ti-is-'a]	*Ninth*	= [ti-su-'u]
10	=	⟨	'e-sir-tu, 'es-e-rit, 'es-rit	'es-ru	*Tenth*	= ['es-ru]
11	=	⟨⟨	[estinesru ?] ...			

15	=	𒐏	...	...	...	kha-mis-se-rit
20	=	𒌋𒌋	...	...	...	es-ra-'a
30	=	𒌍	...	...	...	si-la-sa-'a
40	=	𒐏	...	...	...	ir-ba-'a, ir-ba-ya
50	=	𒐐	...	...	...	kha-an-sa-'a
60	=	𒁹	...	...	...	sus-su
70	=	𒁹𒌋	...	...	...	[śi-bu-'a ?]
80	=	𒁹𒌋𒌋	...	...	...	?
90	=	𒁹𒌍	...	...	...	?
100	=	𒈨	...	...	...	me'
1000	=	𒌋𒈨	...	...	...	a-la-pu

EXAMPLE :   𒐖 𒌋𒈨 𒐏 𒈨 𒐐𒁹 𒁹𒌋𒐊 = " 2,451 oxen."

In writing " one " we sometimes find the phonetic complement added to the cipher to denote whether it has the masculine or the feminine form.   Thus, 𒁹 (EST-*en*) = *estin*, 𒁹 (IKII-*it*) = *ikhit*.

Fractional numbers are as follows :— 𒀸𒁹 *su-un-nu* (ideographically written 𒑰) = " one-half," 𒁹 𒊺𒁹 *su-us-sa-a-nu* = " one-third," 𒌋 *si-ni-bu* = " two-thirds," 𒊺𒁹 *pa-ra-pu* = " five-sixths," 𒐊 *ru-bu* = " one-fourth," 𒊺𒁹 *śu-du* = " one-sixth," 𒊺𒁹 *śu-ma-nu* = " one-eighth," and 𒁹 𒊺𒁹 *su-us-su* = " a sixtieth."

The adverbial numerals were formed by the termination *yānu*, as 𒊺𒁹 *sa-ni-e-'ā-nu*, or 𒊺𒁹 *sa-ni-ya-a-nu* " a second time " (" twice "), *sal-si-'a-nu* or *sal-si-ya-a-nu* " a third time." 𒊺𒁹 *sa-ni-tu* (" repetition ") was used for " once," and in the later inscriptions it took the place of the adverbial numerals, e.g., *sa-ni-ti sal-sa* " the third time." *Sal-sa* is expressed in the Behistun inscription by the compound ideograph 𒑰.

Among the indefinite numerals may be reckoned 𒊺𒁹 *ca-lu*, 𒊺𒁹 *ca-la*, 𒊺𒁹 *cal*, 𒊺𒁹 *cul-lat* " all," 𒊺𒁹 *gab-bu* " all," 𒊺𒁹 *gim-ru* " the whole," 𒊺𒁹 *ma'-du-tu* " much," and 𒊺𒁹 *ca-bit-tu* " much."

THE PRONOUNS.

THE PERSONAL PRONOUNS:—

1. Sing.	𒀭𒀀𒆪 or 𒀀𒆪	anacu... ...	= *I*
„	yāti ... ... yātima ...	}= *I*
Plural	a-[nakh?]-ni	= *we*
2. Sing. Masc....	atta	= *thou*
„ Fem. ...	atti	= *thou*
Com. Gend....	cātu ... ... cāta	}= *thou*
Plural, Masc....	attunu ...	= *you*
„ Fem. ...	[at-ti-na] ...	= *you*
3. Sing. Masc. ...	sū	= *he, it, him*
Fem. ...	sī	= *she, it, her*
Plural, Masc....	sūnu ... ... sun ... ... sunūtu ... sunūti ... sunūt ...	= *they, them*
„ Fem. ...	sina ... ... sin ... ... sināti	= *they, them*

Yā-ti (*yā-ti-ma*) and *cātu* (*cā-ta*) are more substantival in their use than the other forms of the first two personal pronouns, and are generally met with as the first words of a sentence. Besides *yā-ti* we also find ▷◁𐫀 ⟨𐫀- *yā-si* and 𐫀𐫀 ⟨𐫀- *ai-si*.

The Possessive Pronouns are suffixed to the Nouns and Verbs. The following is a list of them:—

POSSESSIVE PRONOUN AFFIXES OF THE NOUN.

1.	*Sing. Com. Gend.*		ya, ā ... ... = *my; also* i, *as* 𐫀 𐫀 *to be read* 'āb-i, *my father*
	Plural „		ni ... ...⎫ nu ... ...⎭ = *our*
2.	*Sing. Masc.* ...		ca, *also* -c ... = *thy*
	„ *Fem.* ...		ci ... ... = *thy*
	Plural, Masc. ...		cunu, *also* cun = *your*
	„ *Fem.* ...		[cina] ... ... = *your*
3.	*Sing. Masc.* ...		su, *also* -s ... = *his, its*
	„ *Fem.* ...		sa ... ...⎫ si ... ...⎭ = *her, its*
	Plural, Masc. ...		sunu, *also* sun = *their*
	„ *Fem.* ...		sina, *also* sin... = *their*

Ya and *ā* were used as the pronoun suffix of the first person if the noun terminated in a vowel, *i* if it terminated in a consonant.

When the noun ends in *d, dh, t, s, s̀, z,* or *ts,* the third person suffix becomes *s̀u, s̀a,* &c., as *khi-ri-it-s̀u* "its ditch," *bit-s̀u* "his house." The last letter of the noun is very frequently assimilated to the *s̀* of the suffix, as *khi-ri-is̀-s̀u, bis̀-su;* and then the reduplication may be dropped, so that we get *khi-ri-s̀u, bi-s̀u.*

In the later period of the language, the possessive pronouns are attached to the substantive *at-tu* "being" or "essence," and the compound is then used as an emphatic repetition of the pronoun; thus ⟨cuneiform⟩ *zir-ya at-tū-a* = "my own race" (literally "my race (which is) mine"), ⟨cuneiform⟩ *at-tu-u-à, a-bu-u-a* "to me (was) my father."

When the accent fell on the last vowel of the noun to which the possessive pronoun was suffixed, the initial consonant of the second and third pronoun suffixes were often doubled, as ⟨cuneiform⟩ *cir-bu-us-su* "its interior," for *cirbú-su*.

POSSESSIVE PRONOUN SUFFIXES OF THE VERB.

1.	*Sing.*		-anni, -inni, -nni, -ni ...	... *Plural*	-annini, -annu, -nini, -nu
2.	„	*Masc.*	-acca, -icca, -cca, -ca, -c ...	„	-accunu, -accun, -cunu, -cun
2.	„	*Fem.*	-acci, -icci, -cci, -ci	„	-accina, -accin, -cina, -cin
3.	„	*Masc.*	-assu, -issu, -su, -s	„	-assunuti, -assunu, -assun, -sunutu (v), -sunuti (v), -sunuta (v), -sunu, -sun
3.	„	*Fem.*	-assi, -assa, -ssa, -ssi, -sa, -si ...	„	-assinati, -assina, -assin, -sinatu (v), sinati (v), -sinata (v), -sina, -sin

A final *n* might be assimilated to the *initial s* of the 3rd person suffix; thus ⟨cuneiform⟩ *in-da-na-as-su-nu-ti* "he gave them," for *indanan-sunuti*.

Besides -*cunu*, we also find ⟨cuneiform⟩ *cu-nu-ti*, and besides ⟨cuneiform⟩ *sunuti* and ⟨cuneiform⟩ *sinati*, we find *su-nu-siv* or *su-nu-si* and *si-na-si-iv*, just as *yāsi* appears by the side of *yāti*. *An-na-si* (*na-si*), "us," occurs in the account of the Deluge, col. iv., line 26.

THE DEMONSTRATIVE PRONOUNS.

	Sing.			*Plural.*	
Masc. ... 𒂎 𒈨 𒈨	su'atu, su'ati, su'ata = *this, that* ...	𒈨 𒈨 𒈨 𒌋	su'atunu, su'atun, sātunu
Fem. ... 𒈨 𒈨 𒈨	si'atu, ...		
„ ... 𒈨 𒈨 𒈨	sa'atu (*or* sātu), ... sa'ati, sa'ata ...	𒈨 𒈨 𒈨 𒌋	su'atina, satina, sinatina
Masc. ... 𒈨 𒈨	sa'asu, *or* sāsu = *this, that*... 𒈨 𒌋	sāsunu, sāsun
Fem. ... 𒈨 𒈨	sa'asa *or* sāsa, sa'asi ... *or* sāsi	... 𒈨 𒈨 𒈨 𒌋 sa'asina *or* sāsina

Three demonstratives are used to determinate distance, 𒄠 *ammu* or 𒈨 *ma* ("hic") "this by me;" 𒀭 *annu* ("iste") "that by you;" and 𒌌 *'ullu* ("ille") "that by him." Of *ammu* we find only the sing. fem. 𒄠 𒈨 𒈨 *ammāte*, and *mā* (𒈨 𒈨) or *ma* the contracted form of the sing. masc. *amma*, and the pl. masc. *ammūta*, which is used as a suffix. Thus we have *śar Assur-ma*, "king of this same Assyria;" *anni-ma* or *an-ma*, "myself" (literally, "this person here"); 𒈨 𒄠 𒈨 𒈨 𒈨 *ina sanati-ma si'ati* "in this very year." This suffix is especially common at the end of the astrological tablets.

Sing. Masc..... an-nu	*Plural, Masc.*.... an-nu-tu, an-nu-tav, an-ni-e
„ „ ... an-ni-i, an-ni, a-an-ni	„ „ ... an-nu-ti
„ „ ... an-na-a, an-na	
„ *Fem.* ... an-nă-tu, a-a-na-ti	„ *Fem.* ... an-na-a-ti, an-nā-tav, an-nī-ti
„ „ ... [an-nĭ-tu]	„ „ ... an-ne-tav, an-ni-tav, an-ni-ti
„ *Masc.*.... ul-lu	„ *Masc.*.... ul-lu-tu
„ „ ... ul-li, ul-li-e	
„ „ ... ul-la	
„ *Fem.* ... ul-lă-tu	„ *Fem.* ... [ul-la-a-tu]

From *ullu* was formed in later times the adj. 𒀉𒉿 𒂊𒈨 𒉌 𒉌 *ulluai* "on the further side."

In the Persian period we find a new demonstrative '*aga*, or *haga*, or *hagat* :

Sing. Masc. ... 𒉌 𒂊𒌅 '*aga*, '*a-ga-a*, *a-ga-h* ... *Com. gen.* ... 𒉌 𒂊𒌅 𒉌 '*a-ga-a*

„ *Fem.* ... 𒉌 𒂊𒌅 𒈾𒋾 '*a-gă-ta*

This pronoun was further compounded with *annu* and the personal pronouns, so as to strengthen the determinative idea ; thus :

Singular, Masc. ... 𒉌 𒂊𒌅 𒉡 '*agannu*, '*aganna*

„　　„ ... 𒉌 𒂊𒌅 𒋗 𒋗 '*aga-su'u*, *he namely*

Plural, Masc. ... 𒉌 𒂊𒌅 𒉡 𒈨𒌍 '*agannutu*, *aganutu*

„　*Fem.* ... 𒉌 𒂊𒌅 𒉡 𒊹 𒈨𒌍 '*agannitu*, '*aganet*

„　　„ ... 𒉌 𒂊𒌅 𒋗 𒉡 '*aga-sunu*, *they namely*

Instead of '*aga-sū*, *sū-aga* also occurs, and *aga* is frequently used like a mere article.

RELATIVE PRONOUNS.

The Relative Pronoun is 𒁹 *sa*, of all numbers and genders, which was originally a demonstrative. It may be understood, as in English, "the man I saw" for "the man *whom* I saw." It is often used to express the periphrastic genitive, when instead of the construct state, the full form of the first noun with the case-ending is given followed by *sa*, which then means exactly our "of." Thus 𒀭𒁹 *šarru sa matâti* "king of the world." Sometimes the first noun was omitted, as *ina sa Gargamis* "according to (the maneh) of Carchemish."

The Interrogative Pronoun is 𒀭 *man-nu*, 𒀭 *mā-nu*, or 𒀭 *man*, "who?" "what," "which." Sometimes it is contracted into *ma-a*. *Mi-e* or *mi* also signified "who," and may be suffixed to *mannu*, forming 𒀭 *mannu-me*, "who."

The Indefinite Pronouns are the indeclinable 𒀭 *ma-nam-ma*, *ma na-ma, man-ma, ma-am-man, ma-am-ma*, or *ma-num-ma*, "anybody," and 𒀭 *mi-im-ma*, "anything." The negative 𒀭 *la* or 𒀭 *ul*, joined in the same sentence with these pronouns, gave them a negative meaning, "nobody," "nothing." This negative meaning might be retained even when the accompanying negative was dropped, like *personne*, &c., in French. 𒀭 *ai-um-ma* or *ya-um-ma*, with the negative understood, and 𒀭 *nin* also, signified "nobody." 𒀭 *matina* was "at any time," or "in any place." The indeclinable 𒀭 *mala* = "as many as." "Some, others," was expressed by 𒀭 *ā-nu-te—ā-nu-te*, and 𒀭 *a-kha-di—a-kha-di*. *A-kha-ri-tu* = "other," *sa-num-ma* = "another," *estin ana estin* = "one to another."

The Reflexive Pronoun is 𒀭 *ra-ma-nu, ra-ma-ni, ra-ma-na* "self," to which the possessive pronouns were suffixed, as *ra-ma-ni-ya* "myself," *ra-ma-nu-ca* or *ra-ma-nu-uc-ca* "thyself," *ra-ma-ni-su-un* "themselves." 𒀭 *gadu* also was used for "individual," and "myself" might be expressed by 𒀭 *an-ni-ma* or 𒀭 *an-ma* (literally "this (man) here ").

THE VERB.

Assyrian Verbs are for the most part triliteral, that is to say, the root consists of three consonants or semi-consonants.

If the root consist of three consonants the verb is called *complete;* if one or more of the three radical letters are semi-consonants which easily pass into vowels (*h* or ‫א‬ becoming *a; v* or ‫ו‬ becoming *u; y* or ‫י‬ becoming *i;* and *e* or ‫ע‬ losing its guttural sound), the verb is called *defective.*

There are four principal Conjugations :—

(1) Kal, the simplest form, with an active (more rarely a neuter) signification, as ►╎‹╎‹ ⟨▦⟩ *ictum* "he concealed."

(2) Niphal, the passive of Kal, formed by prefixing *n*, which may be assimilated to the following vowel, as ►╎‹╎‹ ►⊏╞╎ ⟨▦⟩ *iccatum* "he was concealed" (for *incatum*).

(3) Pael, with an intensive (and hence, sometimes a causative) signification, formed by doubling the second radical letter of the root, and conjugating the persons with an inserted *u*, as ⊨╎╎╎⊨ ⊒╎ ⟨▦⟩ *yucattum* (=*i-u-cattum*) "he did conceal."

(4) Shaphel, with a causative signification, formed by prefixing *s(a)* to the root, and conjugating the persons with inserted *u*, as ⊨╎╎╎⊨ ►╎╎⫤ ⟨▦⟩ *yusactum* "he caused to conceal."

Instead of Shaphel, concave verbs [*see below*] have *Aphel, s* having been changed into *h* and lost, as ⊨╎╎╎⊨ ◁ ╞╎╎ *yudhib* "he caused to be good."

Each of the four principal conjugations has two secondary forms made by inserting *t* and *tan* after the first consonant; thus :—

(1*a*) Iphteal from Kal, as ►╎‹╎‹ ⊨⊑╎╎╎ ⟨▦⟩ *ic-ta-tum.*

(1*b*) Iphtaneal from Kal, as ►╎‹╎‹ ⊨╎╎╎ ⟨▦⟩ *ic-tan-tum.*

(2a)   Ittaphal from Niphal, as 𒀲 𒈬 𒀭 *it-ta-ctum* (for *in-ta-ctum*).

(2b)   Ittanaphal from Niphal, as 𒀲 𒈬 𒀸 𒀀 𒈬 𒀭 *it-tan- -accatum* (for *in-tan-accatum*).

(3a)   Iphtaal from Pael, as 𒀸 𒈬 𒈨 𒀭 *yuc-ta-ttum*.

(3b)   Iphtanaal from Pael, as 𒀸 𒈬 𒀸 𒈨 𒀭 *yuc-tan-altum*.

(4a)   Istaphal from Shaphel, as 𒄑 𒈬 𒀭 *yus-ta-ctum* or *yul-ta-ctum*.

(4b)   Istanaphal from Shaphel, as 𒄑 𒈬 𒀸 𒀀 𒀭 *yus-tan-actum* or *yul-tan-actum*.

From the Aphel of concave verbs is formed an Itaphal, as 𒂊 𒈬 𒂊 *yu-ta-dhib*.

These secondary conjugations have a reflexive force.

Niphal and Shaphel (and also probably Aphel) admit also of *Paelised* conjugations, (2c) Niphael, as 𒀸 𒈨 𒀭 *iccattum*, and (4c) Shaphael, as 𒄑 𒈨 𒀭 *yuscattum*.

From Niphal, Pael, and Shaphel, other intensive conjugations could be formed by repeating the last radical : thus (2nd) Niphalel, as 𒀸 𒀸 𒈨 𒀸 𒀸 *iccatumĭm*; (3rd) Palel, as *yucatumĭm*; and (4th) Shaphalel, as *yusactumĭm*.

Except Kal and Niphal, which stood in the relation of active and passive to one another, the other conjugations had passives formed by changing the vowels of the root into *u*, thus :

(3)   Pael makes 𒂊 𒈨 𒀸 𒀭 *yucuttum* (permansive, *cuttum*).

(4)   Shaphel makes 𒄑 𒈨 𒀭 *yus-cu-tum* (permansive, *sucutum* or *sucatum*).

   Aphel makes 𒂊 𒈨 𒂊 *yudhub*.

(4a)   Istaphal makes (permansive) 𒈨 𒈬 𒀸 𒀸 *sutactim*.

The MOODS are five in number—(1) the indicative, (2) the subjunctive, (3) the imperative, (4) the precative, and (5) the infinitive.

The indicative possesses two primary and three secondary TENSES—(1) the permansive or perfect; (2) the aorist or imperfect; (3) the present, a modified form of the aorist; (4) the perfect or pluperfect, the older form of the aorist; and (5) the future, the older form of the present.

The original tenses of the verb were (1) the perfect (permansive) and (2) the imperfect (aorist); but under the influence of Accadian, the imperfect split itself into two forms, one shorter (as 𒀭 𒀀 𒈾 *iscun* "he made") and one longer (as 𒂊 𒀭 𒈾 *isaccin* "he makes"), which came to be used with a real tense-distinction of meaning (as in Ethiopic). The longer and more primitive form of the present (*isaccinu*) came further to be used with a future force; and the longer and more primitive form of the aorist (*iscunu*), from its being adopted after words like "when" or "who," came to have generally a perfect or pluperfect sense.

The permansive (perfect) has grown out of the close attachment of abbreviated forms of the personal pronouns to nouns and participles into a true tense.

Besides the apocopated or ordinary aorist (*iscun*) and the pluperfect aorist (*iscunu*), there exists (1) a conditional or motive aorist (*iscuna*) formed by the attachment of *a*, "the augment of motion," to the apocopated aorist, and (2) the energic aorist formed by the retention of the original mimmation, *iscunum(ma)*, *iscunim(ma)*, *iscunam(ma)*. There was also another form of the aorist which ended in -*i* (as *iscuni*).

These terminations of the aorist in -*u*, -*i*, -*a*, answer to the three case-endings of the noun, the apocopated aorist corresponding with the construct state, and go back to a time when but little distinction was made between the noun and the verb. The subjunctive mood is used in relative and conditional clauses, and is denoted by the addition of the particle *ni*, which may be placed after the possessive pronoun suffix, as 𒅖 𒂊 𒀀 𒈾 𒌋 *ci ikabu-su-ni* "when he had called it."

The imperative is confined to the 2nd person, the 2nd pers. sing. masc. giving the simplest form of the verb (as *sucun*, *rikhits*, *tsabat*), the vowels always being the same in both syllables, the 2nd pers. fem. ending in *i* (as *sucini* or *sucni*), the 2nd pers. pl. masc. in *-u* (as *sucinu* or *sucnu*) and the 2nd pers. pl. fem. in *ā* (as *sucinā* or *sucnā*). The 2nd pers. sing. masc. may take the augment of motion *-ă* (as *sucună* or *sucnă*). The precative is formed by prefixing *lu* or *li* (the vowel of which coalesces with the vowel of the person-prefix in the 1st and 3rd persons) to any one of the forms of the aorist. It is generally used in the 3rd person, as *liscun* "may he place." The infinitive is really a verbal substantive and declined accordingly.

Besides the moods, every conjugation possesses a participle, which, except in Kal and the Pael of concave verbs, prefixes *mu-*.

There are three *numbers*, singular, plural, and dual, but the dual which ends in *-ā* is only found in the 3rd person.

There are three Persons in the singular and plural, the 2nd and 3rd having different forms for masculine and feminine.

A feminine nominative, however, is often used improperly with a masculine verb (as 𒀭 𒈹 𒁹𒁹𒁹 ⚒𒇻𒀭 *Istar yusapri* "the goddess Istar disclosed") and on the other hand, in the 2nd pers. plural (especially in the imperative) we frequently find the feminine instead of the masculine form.

There are many contracted forms in the Assyrian verb, produced chiefly by dropping a short *-ĭ* or *-ă*; thus 𒁹 𒁹 𒁹 *tastalmi* for *tastalami*, 𒁹 𒁹 𒁹 *taptikdi* for *taptikidi*, *ittalcu* for *ittallicu*, *tasalmu* for *tasallimu*, *usziz* or *ulziz* for *usaziz*.

D, *ts*, *z*, or *s* assimilate the inserted *t* of the secondary conjugations, as 𒁹 𒁹 𒁹 *its-tsa-bat* for 𒁹 𒁹 𒁹 *its-ta-bat*, 𒁹 𒁹 𒁹 *iz-za-car* for *iz-ta-car*.

S may change the *t* into *š* becoming *š* itself, as 𒁹 𒁹 𒁹 *iš-ša-can* and *i-ša-can* for 𒁹 𒁹 𒁹 *is-ta-can*.

The enclitic conjunction *vă* ("and)" is attached very closely to the termination of the verb.

The vowel of the syllable which follows the first radical in the aorist and present is sometimes weakened to *i* or *e*, through assimilation to the vowel of the next syllable; as 𒁹 𒁹 𒁹 𒁹 *i-ve-eš-sir*, "he abandons;" 𒁹 𒁹 𒁹 𒁹 *yu-se-pi-ic*, "he heaped up;" 𒁹 𒁹 𒁹 𒁹 *yu-se-ec-nis*, "he caused to submit;" 𒁹 𒁹 𒁹 *yup-te-kid*, "he overlooked;" 𒁹 𒁹 𒁹 𒁹 *i-se-er-ri*, "he stretches;" 𒁹 𒁹 𒁹 𒁹 *ip-pi-sid-du*, "they were extended."

PARADIGMS.

The Strong or Complete Verb.

KAL.

The second vowel of the aorist may be either *a*, *i*, or *u*, as *iscun* "he placed," *ipdhir* "he freed," *itsbat* "he took," but *u* is most common.

The third vowel of the present may similarly be either *a*, *i*, or *u*, as *inaccar* "he estranges," *isaccin* "he places," *idammum* "it passes away," but *i* is, by far, the most common vowel.

The first person singular of the aorist sometimes has *e* in Babylonian instead of *a*, as ⟪⟪ 𒀭𒌋 *esnik* for *asnik*, and verbs א"פ (see *infra*) in Assyrian might adopt the same vowel.

PERMANSIVE [*or* Perfect].—*Singular.*				PRESENT.—*Singular.*		
1.	𒑒𒑒 𒑒𒑒		sac-na-cu *or* sac-na-ac	𒑒 𒑒𒑒 𒑒	a-sac-cin "*I place*"
2. *Masc.*	„	„	sac-na at	„	„	ta-sac-cin
2. *Fem.*	„	„	sac-na-at	„	„	ta-sac-ci-ni
3. *Masc.*	„	„	sa-cin (𒑒 𒑒)	„	„	i-sac-cin
3. *Fem.*	„	„	sac-na-a-at (sacnāt)	„	„	ta-sac-cin

	Plural.				*Plural.*	
1.	„	„	?	𒑒𒑒 𒑒	ni-sac-cin
2. *Masc.*	„	„	sac-na-tu-nu	„	„	ta-sac-ci-nu
2. *Fem.*	„	„	[? sac-na-ti-na]	„	„	ta-sac-ci-na
3. *Masc.*	„	„	sac-nu	„	„	i-sac-ci-nu
3. *Fem.*	„	„	sac-na	„	„	i-sac-ci-na

	Dual.				*Dual.*	
3.	𒑒𒑒 𒑒𒑒	sac-na-a [sacnā] ...		„	„	[i-sac-ci-na-a]

AORIST.

Singular.

1.	𒀸𒋢𒌦 as-cun ("*I placed*");		𒅈𒄭𒄑 ar-khi-its ("*I inundated*");		𒀜𒌑 ·ats-bat ("*I took*")	
2. *Masc.*	„ „ tas-cun;	„	„ tar-khi-its;	„	„	ta-ats-bat
2. *Fem.*	„ „ tas-cu-ni;	„	„ tar-khi-tsi;	„	„	ta-ats ba-ti
3. *Masc.*	„ „ is-cun;	„	„ ir-khi-its;	„	„	its-bat
3. *Fem.*	„ „ tas-cun;	„	„ tar-khi-its;	„	„	ta-ats-bat

Plural.

1.	𒉌𒅖 ni-is-cun;		𒉌𒅕 ni-ir-khi-its;		𒉌 ni-its-bat	
2. *Masc.*	„ „ tas-cu-nu;	„	„ tar-khi-tsu;	„	„	ta-ats-ba-tu
2. *Fem.*	„ „ tas-cu-na;	„	„ tar-khi-tsa;	„	„	ta-ats-ba-ta
3. *Masc.*	„ „ is-cu-nu;	„	„ ir-khi-tsu;	„	„	its-ba-tu
3. *Fem.*	„ „ is-cu-na;	„	„ ir-khi-tsa;	„	„	its-ba-ta

Dual.

3.	𒅖𒌋𒈾 { is-cu-na-a [iscunā]; }	𒅕𒄭𒉌𒉌 ir-khi-tsa-a;		𒄿𒁀𒋫𒀀 its-ba-ta-a

The student will form the future and pluperfect by attaching the vowel -*u* to those singular forms of the present and aorist which end in a consonant, and -*uni* (also -*unu*, -*unuv*, and -*univ*) to those plural forms of the same tenses which end in a consonant.

IMPERATIVE.

Sing.	2. *Masc.*	𒁲𒋢𒌦 su-cun;		𒊑𒄭𒄑 ri-khi-its;		𒀜𒌑 tsa-bat		
„	2. *Fem.*	„ „ su-ci-ni *or* su-uc-ni;	„	„ ri-khi-tsi *or* ri-ikh-tsi;	„	tsa-ba-ti *or* tsa-ab-ti		
Plu.	2. *Masc.*	„ „ su-ci-nu *or* su-uc-nu;	„	„ ri-khi-tsu *or* ri-ikh-tsu;	„	tsa-ba-tu *or* tsa-ab-tu		
„	2. *Fem.*	„ „ su-ci-na *or* su-uc-na;	„	„ ri-khi-tsa *or* ri-ikh-tsa;	„	tsa-ba-ta *or* tsa-ab-ta		

PRECATIVE.

Singular.

1.　🔲🔲🔲🔲🔲 lu-us-cun;　🔲🔲🔲🔲 lu-ur-khi-its;　🔲🔲🔲 lu-uts-bat

2. *Masc.*　„　„　lu-tas-cun;　„　„　lu-tar-khi-its;　„　„　lu-ta-ats-bat

3. *M. & F.*　„　„　li-is-cun;　„　„　li-ir-khi-its;　„　„　li-its-bat

Plural.

3. *Masc.*　🔲🔲🔲🔲 li-is-cu-nu;　🔲🔲🔲🔲 li-ir-khi-tsu;

3. *Fem.*　„　„　li-is-cu-na;　„　„　li-ir-khi-tsa;

3. *Masc.*　🔲🔲🔲🔲 li-its-ba-tu

3. *Fem.*　„　„　li-its-ba-ta

The augment of motion and the mimmation may be attached to all the above forms. When the augment of motion is attached to the 2nd person masc. plur. of the imperative *u+a* passes through *va* into *ā* ; thus 🔲🔲🔲🔲 *su-uc-nā* (or 🔲🔲🔲 *su-uc-na-a*) instead of *su-uc-nu-a*.

INFINITIVE.		PARTICIPLE.	
🔲🔲🔲 sā-cā-nu	*to dwell.*	🔲🔲🔲 sā-ci-nu	*dwelling.*
🔲🔲🔲 ra-kha-tsu	*to inundate.*	🔲🔲🔲 rā-khi-tsu	*inundating.*
🔲🔲🔲 tsa-ba-tu	*to seize.*	🔲🔲🔲 tsā-bi-tu	*seizing.*

IPHTEAL.

	PERMANSIVE (Perfect).				PRESENT.	
	Singular.				*Singular.*	
1.	𒊓𒌅𒈾𒅗 sit-cu-na-cu ...				𒀸𒋫𒃷 as-tac-can	
					𒀸𒋫𒃷 as-ta-can	
					𒀠𒋫𒃷 al-ta-can	
2. *Masc.*	,,	,,	[sit-cu-na-at] ...	,,	,,	tas-tac-can, &c.
2. *Fem.*	,,	,,	?	,,	,,	tas-tac-ca-ni
3. *Masc.*	,,	,,	sit-cun ...	,,	,,	is-tac-can
3. *Fem.*	,,	,,	sit-cu-nat ...	,,	,,	tas-tac-can
	Plural.				*Plural.*	
1.	,,	,,	?	𒐲𒋫𒃷 nis-tac-can		
2. *Masc.*	,,	,,	?	,,	,,	tas-tac-ca-nu
2. *Fem.*	,,	,,	?	,,	,,	tas-tac-ca-na
3. *Masc.*	,,	,,	sit-cu-nu ...	,,	,,	is-tac-ca-nu
3. *Fem.*	,,	,,	sit-cu-na ...	,,	,,	is-tac-ca-na
	Dual.				*Dual.*	
3.	,,	,,	[sit-cu-na-a] ...	[is-tac-ca-na-a]		

AORIST.

	Singular.					
1.	𒀸𒋫𒐼𒃷 as-ta-cin, al-ta-cin ;			𒀊𒋼𒅗 ap-te-kid *"I overlooked"*		
2. *Masc.*	,,	,,	tas-ta-cin, &c.;	,,	,,	ta-ap-te-kid
3. *Fem.*	,,	,,	tas-ta-ci-ni ;	,,	,,	ta-ap-te-ki-di
3. *Masc.*	,,	,,	is-ta-cin ;	,,	,,	ip-te-kid
3. *Fem.*	,,	,,	tas-ta-cin ;	,,	,,	ta-ap-te-kid
	Plural.					
1.	𒐲𒋫𒐼𒃷 nis-ta-cin ;			�níi-ip-te-kid		
2. *Masc.*	,,	,,	tas-ta-ci-nu ;	,,	,,	ta-ap-te-ki-du
2. *Fem.*	,,	,,	tas-ta-ci-na ;	,,	,,	tap-te-ki-da
3. *Masc.*	,,	,,	is-ta-ci-nu ;	,,	,,	ip-te-ki-du
3. *Fem.*	,,	,,	is-ta-ci-na ;	,,	,,	ip-te-ki-da
	Dual.					
3.	,,	,,	[is-ta-ci-na-a]	,,	,,	[ip-te-ki-da-a]

IPHTEAL—*continued.*

IMPERATIVE.

	Singular.			Plural.	
2. *Masc.*	𒋾𒁷	sit-cin, patkid		𒋾𒈾𒌋	sit-ci-nu
2. *Fem.*	,, ,,	sit-ci-ni		,, ,,	sit-ci-na

PRECATIVE.
Singular.

1.		lu-us-ta-can ;		lu-up-te-kid
3.	,, ,,	li-is-ta-can ;	,, ,,	li-ip-te-kid

Plural.

3. *M.*		li-is-ta-ca-nu ;		li-ip-te-ki-du
3. *F.*	,, ,,	li-is-ta-ca-na ;	,, ,,	li-ip-te-ki-da

INFINITIVE.

sit-cu-nu ; pit-ku-du

PARTICIPLE.

mus-ta-ca-nu, mul-ta-ca-nu

mu-up-te-ki-du

NIPHAL.

PERMANSIVE (Perfect).		
Singular.		
1.	... ...	[na-as-cu-na-cu]
2. *Masc.*	... ...	[na-as-cu-na-at]
2. *Fem.*	... ... ?	
3. *Masc.*	⟨cuneiform⟩	na-as-cun
3. *Fem.*	„ „	[na-as-cu-nat]

Plural.		
1.	? „ „	
2. *Masc.*	? „ „	
2. *Fem.*	? „ „	
3. *Masc.*	⟨cuneiform⟩	na-as-cu-nu
3. *Fem.*	„ „	na-as-cu-na

Dual.		
3	... ...	[na-as-cu-na-a]

PRESENT.		
Singular.		
⟨cuneiform⟩		as-sa-can
„	„	tas-sa-can
„	„	tas-sa-ca-ni
„	„	is-sa-ca-an
„	„	tas-sa-can

Plural.		
⟨cuneiform⟩		ni-is-sa-can
„	„	tas-sa-ca-nu
„	„	tas-sa-ca-na
⟨cuneiform⟩		is-sa-ca-nu
„	„	is-sa-ca-na

Dual.		
„	„	[is-sa-ca-na-a]

IMPERATIVE.		
Singular.		
2. *Masc.*	⟨cuneiform⟩	na-as-cin
2. *Fem.*	„ „	na-as-ci-ni

Plural.		
2. *Masc.*	„ „	na-as-ci-nu
2. *Fem.*	„ „	na-as-ci-na

PRECATIVE.		
Singular.		
1.	⟨cuneiform⟩	lu-us-sa-cin
3.	„ „	li-is-sa-cin

Plural.		
3. *Masc.*	„ „	lis-sa-ci-nu, lis-sac-nu
3. *Fem.*	„ „	lis-sa-ci-na, lis-sac-na

AORIST.		
Singular.		
1.	⟨cuneiform⟩	as-sa-cin, as-sa-cun
2. *Masc.*	„ „	tas-sa-cin, tas-sa-cun
2. *Fem.*	„ „	tas-sa-ci-ni, tas-sa-cu-ni
3. *Masc.*	„ „	is-sa-cin, is-sa-cun
3. *Fem.*	„ „	tas-sa-cin, tas-sa-cun

AORIST—*Continued.*

Plural.

1.	𒀭 𒇹 𒅆 𒊓𒇹	na-as-sa-cin, na-as-sa-cun
2. *Masc.*	„	„	tas-sa-ci-nu, tas-sa-cu-nu
2. *Fem.*	„	„	tas-sa-ci-na, tas-sa-cu-na
3. *Masc.*	„	„	is-sa-ci-nu, is-sa-cu-nu
3. *Fem.*	„	„	is-sa-ci-na, is-sa-cu-na

Dual.

3	„	„	[is-sa-ci-na-a]

INFINITIVE.

𒀭 𒇹 𒅖 𒇽 𒈾 na-as-ca-a-nu [nascānu]

PARTICIPLE.

𒈦 𒉽 𒌍 𒀭 𒂖 𒈾 mu-se-es-sa-ci-nu [musessacinu]

ITTAPHAL.

PERMANSIVE (*or* Perfect).
Singular.

1. [na-as-te-cu-na-cu?], &c.   ...   ...

PRESENT.
Singular.

1. 𒀭𒈾𒊨𒃶 at-ta-as-can, &c.

IMPERATIVE.
Singular.

2. *Masc.* ni-tas-cin (?), &c.   ...   .

PRECATIVE.
Singular.

3.   „   „   li-it-tas-cin, &c.

AORIST.
Singular.

1. 𒀭𒈾𒊨𒃶 at-ta-as-cin
    at-ta-as-cun, &c.

INFINITIVE.
na-at-sa-cā-nu

PARTICIPLE.
mut-tas-ca-nu

PAEL.

	PERMANSIVE (*or* Perfect). *Singular.*				PRESENT *Singular.*	
1.	𒊬𒂵𒈾𒋢		sac-ca-na-cu	1.	𒌋𒊬𒃶	u-sac-can
2. *Masc.*	„	„	[sac-ca-na-at]	2. *Masc.*	„ „	tu-sac-can
2. *Fem.*	„	„	?	2. *Fem.*	„ „	tu-sac-ca-ni, tu-sac-ni
3. *Masc.*	𒊬𒃶		sac-can	3. *Masc.*	„ „	yu-sac-can
3. *Fem.*	„		sac-ca-nat	3. *Fem.*	„ „	tu-sac-can

Plural.

					Plural.	
1.	...	?		1.	𒉡𒊬𒃶	nu-sac-can
2. *Masc.*	...	?		2. *Masc.*	„ „	tu-sac-ca-nu
2. *Fem.*	...	?		2. *Fem.*	„ „	tu-sac-ca-na
3. *Masc.*	...	sac-ca-nu		3. *Masc.*	„ „	yu-sac-ca-nu
3. *Fem*	...	[sac-ca-na]		3. *Fem.*	„ „	yu-sac-ca-na

Dual.

				Dual.	
3.	...	[sac-ca-na-a]	3.	„ „	[yu-sac-ca-na-a]

PAEL—*continued.*

IMPERATIVE.			PRECATIVE.		
Singular.			*Singular.*		
2. *Masc.*	𒀸 𒋼	suc-cin (su-cin)	1.	𒂊 𒈨 𒌋	lu-sac-can
2. *Fem.*	„	suc-ci-ni	3.	„ „	lu-sac-can, lu-sac-cin
Plural.			*Plural.*		
2. *Masc.*	𒀸 𒂍 𒌋	suc-ci-nu	3. *Masc.*	𒂊 𒈨 𒂍 𒌋	lu-sac-ca-nu
2. *Fem.*	„	suc-ci-na	3. *Fem.*	„ „	lu-sac-ca-na

			AORIST.				
Singular.					*Plural.*		
1.	𒈨𒌋 𒈨 𒋼	u-sac-cin		1.	𒌋 𒈨 𒋼	nu-sac-cin
		u-sac-cun		2. *Masc.*	„ „	tu-sac-ci-nu
		u-sic-cin		2. *Fem.*	„ „	tu-sac-ci-na
2. *Masc.*	„ „	tu-sac-cin		3. *Masc.*	„ „	yu-sac-ci-nu
		tu-sac-cun		3. *Fem.*	„ „	yu-sac-ci-na
		tu-sic-sin		*Dual.*		
2. *Fem.*	„ „	tu-sac-si-ni, &c.		3.	„ „	[yu-sac-ci-na-a]
3. *Masc.*	„ „	yu-sac-cin				
3. *Fem.*	„ „	tu-sac-cin				

INFINITIVE.			PARTICIPLE.		
𒈨 𒂍 𒌋	sac-cā-nu	[*but the infin. passive is more common*]	𒀸 𒈨 𒂍 𒌋	mu-sac-ci-nu	
Infin. pass.	suc-cu-nu				

From its intensive signification Pael comes sometimes to be used in a causative sense. When Kal is intransitive, Pael is transitive.

N.B.—The present and aorist of Pael are distinguished from the present of Kal by the vowel *u* in the first syllable.

The reduplication is often neglected in writing. It is sometimes replaced in the case of labials and dentals by *mb* (*mp*) and *nd* (*ndh, nt*).

IPHTAEL.

PERMANSIVE.   *Not found.*

PRESENT.

	Singular.			Plural.	
1.	𒌋𒋫𒃷	us-tac-can		𒉡𒌋𒋫𒃷	nu-us-tac-can
2. *Masc.*	„ „	tu-us-tac-can		„ „	tu-us-tac-ca-nu
2. *Fem.*	„ „	tu-us-tac-ca-ni		„ „	tu-us-tac-ca-na
3. *Masc.*	„ „	yus-tac-can		𒌋𒋫𒃷	yus-tac-ca-nu
3. *Fem.*	„ „	tu-us-tac-can		„ „	yus-tac-ca-na

Dual.

„   „   [yus-tac-ca-na-a]

AORIST.

Singular.

1.	𒌋𒋫𒆗	us-tac-cin ;		𒌋𒆪𒁾	up-te-kid
2. *Masc.*	„ „	tu-us-tac-cin ;		„ „	tu-up-te-kid
2. *Fem.*	„ „	tu-us-tac-cin ;		„ „	tu-up-te-ki-di
3. *Masc.*	„ „	yus-tac-cin ;		„ „	yup-te-kid
3. *Fem.*	„ „	tu-us-tac-cin ;		„ „	tu-up-te-kid

Plural.

1.	𒉡𒌋𒋫𒆗	nu-us-tac-cin ;		𒉡𒌋𒆪𒁾	nu-up-te-kid
2. *Masc.*	„ „	tu-us-tac-ci-nu ;		„ „	tu-up-te-ki-du
2. *Fem.*	„ „	tu-us-tac-ci-na ;		„ „	tu-up-te-ki-da
3. *Masc.*	𒌋𒋫𒆗	yus-tac-ci-nu ;		𒌋𒆪𒁾	yup-te-ki-du
3. *Fem.*	„ „	yus-tac-ci-na ;		„ „	yup-te-ki-da

Dual.

3.   „   „   [yus-tac-ci-na-a]

IPHTAEL—*continued*.

IMPERATIVE. *Not found.*

PRECATIVE.

Singular.		*Plural.*	
3. 𒀭𒈾𒋳𒁉 lu-us-tac-can	3. *Masc.* 𒀭𒈾𒋳𒈾 lu-us-tac-ca-nu		
	3. *Fem.* „ „ lu-us-tac-ca-na		

INFINITIVE.	PARTICIPLE.
[sa-tac-cā-nu]	𒈬𒋳𒄭 mus-tac-ci-nu

SHAPHEL.

PERMANSIVE. *Not found.*

	PRESENT.			AORIST.	
	Singular.			*Singular.*	
1.	𒀀𒁄𒁲𒊺𒄿	u-sa-as-can	1.	𒀀𒁲𒊺𒃶	u-sa-as-cin, u-se-es-cin
2. *Masc.*	𒌅𒁲𒊺𒄿	tu-sa-as-can	2. *Masc.*	,, ,,	tu-sa-as-cin, &c.
2. *Fem.*	,, ,,	tu-sa-as-ca-ni	2. *Fem.*	,, ,,	tu-sa-as-ci-ni
3. *Masc.*	,, ,,	yu-sa-as-can	3. *Masc.*	,, ,,	yu-sa-as-cin
3. *Fem.*	,, ,,	tu-sa-as-can	3. *Fem.*	,, ,,	tu-sa-as-cin
	Plural.			*Plural.*	
1.	𒉡𒁲𒊺𒄿	nu-sa-as-can	1.	𒉡𒁲𒊺𒃶	nu-sa-as-cin
2. *Masc.*	,, ,,	tu-sa-as-ca-nu	2. *Masc.*	,, ,,	tu-sa-as-ci-nu
2. *Fem.*	,, ,,	tu-sa-as-ca-na	2. *Fem.*	,, ,,	tu-sa-as-ci-na
3. *M.*	𒀀𒁲𒊺𒈾𒉡	yu-sa-as-ca-nu	3. *Masc.*	., ,,	yu-sa-as-ci-nu
3. *Fem.*	,, ,,	yu-sa-as-ca-na	3. *Fem.*	,, ,,	yu-sa-as-ci-na
	Dual.			*Dual.*	
3.	[yu-sa-as-ca-na-a]		3.	[yu-sa-as-ci-na-a]	

	IMPERATIVE.			PRECATIVE.	
	Singular.			*Singular.*	
2. *Masc.*	𒋗𒍑𒃶	su-us-cin	1.		lu-sa-as-cin
2. *Fem.*	,, ,,	su-us-ci-ni	3.		lu-sa-as-can
	Plural.			*Plural.*	
2. *Masc.*	,, ,,	su-us-ci-nu	3. *M.*	𒇻𒁲𒊺𒄿𒉡	lu-sa-as-ci-nu
2. *Fem.*	,, ,,	su-us-ci-na	3. *Fem.*	,, ,,	lu-sa-as-ci-na

INFINITIVE.

𒁲𒊺𒈾𒉡 sa-as-cā-nu [*but the Infin. passive is more common*].   𒋗𒍑𒄞𒉡 su-us-cu-nu

PARTICIPLE.

𒈬𒁲𒊺𒄿𒉡 mu-sa-as-ci-nu

ISTAPHAL.

PERMANSIVE. *Not found.*

PRESENT.
Singular.

𒈾 𒋾 𒌍   us-tas-can *or*
𒌌 𒋾 𒌍   ul-tas-can,
&c.

AORIST.
Singular.

1. us-tas-cin *or*

ul-tas-cin   𒌌 𒋾 𒌍, {us / ul}-te-sib,
&c.

IMPERATIVE.
Singular.

2. *Masc.* 𒋗 𒋾 𒅖 𒋆   su-ti-is-cin,
&c.

PRECATIVE.
Singular.

3. 𒇻 �us 𒋾 𒌍   lu-us-tas-can,
&c.

INFINITIVE PASSIVE.

𒋗 𒋼 𒌍 𒇴   su-te-es-cu-nu.

PARTICIPLE.

𒈲 𒋾 𒅆 𒉡   mus-tas-ci-nu ;   𒈤 𒋾 𒅆 𒉡   mul-tas-ci-nu.

THE WEAK OR DEFECTIVE VERBS.

If one of the radicals of a verb is *n, á, h, u (v), i (y)* or *e*, it differs in many particulars from the conjugation of the Strong Verb, owing to the assimilation of these letters to other vowels or consonants.

Verbs which begin with these letters are called verbs פ״נ, פ״א, פ״ה, פ״ו, פ״י, and פ״ע; verbs which end with them are called verbs ל״נ, ל״א, ל״ה, ל״י, ל״ו, and ל״ע; verbs which have one of these letters as a second radical are called verbs ע״נ, ע״א, ע״ה, ע״ו, ע״י, and ע״ע. The last class of verbs are also called Concave Verbs.

Verbs פ״נ.

N is assimilated to the following letter; though in some few instances we find it irregularly retained. Before *b* or *p* it may be changed to *m*.

	PERMANSIVE.		PRESENT.
Kal	*(cuneiform)*	na-mir, "*he sees*"	i-nam-mir *or* i-nam-mar
Iphteal	*(cuneiform)*	ni-it-mur	it-ta-mar
Niphal	*(cuneiform)*	nam-mur	in-na-mar
Ittaphal	„ „	[na-at-te-mur]	it-tam-mar
Pael	*(cuneiform)*	nam-mar	yu-nam-mar
Iphtaal	„ „	...	yut-tam-mar
Shaphel	„ „	[sam-mar]	yu-sam-mar
Istaphal	„ „	[sat-ne-mar]	yus-tam-mar
Shaphael	„ „	[sa-nam-mar]	yus-nam-mar
Istaphael	„ „	...	yus-te-nam-mar
	PASSIVE.		PASSIVE.
Pael	*(cuneiform)*	num-mur	yu-num-mar
Iphtaal	„ „	...	yut-tum-mar
Shaphel	*(cuneiform)*	su-nu-mur / su-na-mur	yu-sa-nu-mar
Istaphal	*(cuneiform)*	su-te-nu-mur	yus-tum-mar
Shaphael	*(cuneiform)*	su-num-mur / su-nam-mur	yus-num-mar

		AORIST.			IMPERATIVE.
Kal	...	𒀭�)(	im-mur	"*he saw*"	u-mur *or* a-mur
,,	...		id-din	"*he gave*"	i-din.
,,	...		ip-pal	"*he threw down*"	,, a-pal.
,,	...		e-cil	"*he ate*"	,, e-cil
Iphteal	...		it-ta-mir		,, ni-it-mir
Niphal	...		in-na-mir		,, nam-mir
Ittaphal	...	,,	,, it-tam-mir		,, [ni-tam-mir]
Pael	...	,,	,, yu-nam-mir		,, nu-um-mir
Iphtaal	...	,,	,, yut-tam-mir		—
Shaphel	...	,,	,, yu-sam-mir		,, su-um-mir
Istaphal	...	,,	,, yus-tam-mir		,, su-ut-tim-mir
Shaphael	...	,,	,, yus-nam-mir		,, su-num-mir
Istaphael	...	,,	,, yus-te-nam-mir		—

		PASSIVE.		PASSIVE.
Pael	...		yu-num-mir	—
Iphtaal	...	,,	,, yut-tum-mur	—
Shaphel	...	,,	,, { yu-sa-nu-mur / yus-nu-mur	—
Istaphal	...	,,	,, yus-tum-mur	—
Shaphael	...	,,	,, yus-num-mur	—

		PARTICIPLE.	
Kal	...		nā-mi-ru, nam-ru
Iphteal	...		mut-ta-mi-ru
Niphal	...		mu-un-nam-mi-ru, mun-nam-ru
Ittaphal	...		mut-ta-ma-ru
Pael	...		mu-nam-mi-ru
Iphtaal	...		mut-tam-mi-ru
Shaphel	...		mu-sam-mi-ru
Istaphal	...		mus-tam-mi-ru
Shaphael	...		mus-nam-mi-ru
Istaphael	...		mus-te-nam-mi-ru

Verbs פ״א.

KAL.

PERMANSIVE.	PRESENT.		AORIST.	
Sing. 1. [asabacu]	𒀀𒊍𒂊𒌝	a-sab "*I sit*"	𒆠𒁇 a-sib, 𒂊𒁇 e-sib	
			a-cul, „ e-cul	
„ 2. *Masc.* ... [asabat]	„	ta-sab	„	ta-sib
„ 2. *Fem.* ... —	„	ta-sa-bi	„	ta-si-bi
„ 3. *Masc.* ... [a-sab]	„	ya-sab, i-sab	„	ya-sib, i-sib 𒂊𒁇
„ 3. *Fem.* ... —	„	ta-sab	„	ta-sib
Plur. ... —	𒈾𒊍𒂊𒌝	na-sab	𒈾𒁇	na-sib
„ 2. *Masc.* ... —	„	ta-sa-bu	„	ta-si-bu
„ 2. *Fem.* ... —	„	ta-sa-ba	„	ta-si-ba
„ 3. *Masc.* a-sa-bu, as-bu	„	ya-sa-bu, i-sa-bu	„	ya-si-bu, i-si-bu
„ 3. *Fem.* ... [a-sa-ba]	„	ya-sa-ba, i-sa-ba	„	ya-si-ba, i-si-ba
Dual, 3. ... [asabā]	„	[ya-sa-bā]	„	ya-si-bā]

IMPERATIVE AND PRECATIVE.

Sing. 1. 𒈜𒉌𒅆	li-su-ub, 𒈜𒁇	lu-sib
„ 2. *Masc.* ... „ „	e-sib, a-cul	
„ 2. *Fem.* ... „ „	e-si-bi, a-cu-li	
„ 3. *Masc.* ... „ „	li-su-ub, lu-sib	
„ 3. *Fem.* ... „ „	—	
Plur. 1. ... „ „	—	
„ 2. *Masc.* ... 𒂊𒉌𒊍	e-si-bu, 𒀀𒈜𒅆	a-cu-la
„ 2. *Fem.* ... „ „	e-si-bu, a-cu-la	
„ 3. *Masc.* ... „ „	li-su-bu, lu-si-bu	
„ 3 *Fem.* ... „ „	li-su-ba, lu-si-ba	

INFINITIVE.		PARTICIPLE.	
𒊍𒀀𒊍 ... ... sa-a-bu		𒁇𒉌𒊍 ... ... a-si-bu	

PARADIGM OF THE OTHER CONJUGATIONS.

	PERMANSIVE.				PRESENT.		
Iphteal ...	𒀭 𒂍 𒉿		te-sub		𒂍 𒂊𒐈 𒋻𒅔		i-ta-sab
Niphal ...	„	„	[nā-sub]		„	„	i-na-sab
Ittaphal ...	„	„	—		„	„	it-te-sab
Pael ...	„	„	[assab]		„	„	yu-as-ab, yus-sab
Iphtaal ...	„	„	—		„	„	yu-tas-sab
Shaphel ...	„	„	[sāsab]		„	„	yu-sa-sab, yu-se-sab
Istaphal ...	„	„	[satesab]		„	„	yus-te-sab yul-te-sab
Itaphal ...	„	„	—		„	„	yu-te-sab
Pael Pass. ...	„	„	us-sub		„	„	yu-us-sab
Istaphal Pass.	„	„	su-te-sub		„	„	[yus-tu-sab]

	AORIST.				IMPERATIVE.	PARTICIPLE.		
Iphteal ...	𒂍 𒂊𒐈 𒀀		i-ta-sib		[it-sib]	𒀭 𒂍 𒌋 𒀀		mu-ta-sa-bu
Niphal ...	„	„	i-na-sib		na-sib	„	„	mu-na-si-bu
Ittaphal ...	„	„	it-te-sib		—	„	„	mut-te-si-bu
Pael ...	„	„	yu-as-sib, yus-sib		[us-sib]	„	„	mus-si-bu
Iphtaal ...	„	„	yu-tas-sib		[i-ta-sab]	„	„	mut-tas-sa-bu
Shaphel ...	„	„	yu-sa-sib, yu-se-sib		su-sib	„	„	mu-se-si-bu
Istaphal ...	„	„	yus-te-sib, yul-te-sib		su-te-sib, su-te-sab	„	„	mus-te-si-bu
Itaphal ...	„	„	yu-te-sib		[u-te-sib]	„	„	mu-te-si-bu
Pael Pass.	„	„	yu-us-sub		—	—		
Istaphal Pass.	„	„	[yus-tu-sub]		—	—		

7*

Verbs פ״ה.

KAL.

PERMANSIVE. Singular.		PRESENT. Singular.		AORIST. Singular.	
		𒀠𒇻	al-lac ...	𒀀𒅆	a-lic
1.	[ha-la-ca-cu]	𒀀𒇻	a-lac "I go"	𒀠𒅆	al-lic
		𒀀�------	a-ha-bid "I destroy"	,,	ah-bid
2. *Masc.*	[ha-la--ca-at]	,, ,,	tal-lac, &c. ...	,,	tal-lic, &c.
2. *Fem.*	... ...	,, ,,	tal-la-ci ...	,,	tal-li-ci
3. *Masc.*	𒀀𒇻 ha-lac ...	𒅋𒇻	il-lac ...	𒅋𒅆	il-lic
3. *Fem.*	... ...	,, ,,	tal-lac ...	𒅆	tal-lic
Plural.		*Plural.*		*Plural.*	
1.	... ... '...	,, ,,	na-al-lac ...	,,	na-al-lic
2. *Masc.*	... ...	,, ,,	tal-la-cu ...	,,	tal-li-cu
2. *Fem.*	... ...	,, ,,	tal-la-ca ...	,,	tal-li-ca
3. *Masc.*	ha-la-cu ...	,, ,,	il-la-cu ...	,,	il-li-cu
3. *Fem.*	[ha-la-ca] ...	,, ,,	il-la-ca ...	,,	il-li·ca
Dual.		*Dual.*		*Dual.*	
3.	ha-la-ca-a ...	,, ,,	[illacā] ...	,,	[illicā]

IMPERATIVE AND PRECATIVE.

Singular.			Plural.		
1.	𒀀𒅆	lil-lic	2. *Masc.* ...	𒀠	(h)al-cu
	𒅆	li-lic	2. *Fem.* ...	𒀠	(h)al-ca
2. *Masc.* ...	𒀀𒅆	ha-lic	3. *Masc.* ... ,, ,,		lil-li-cu li-li-cu
2. *Fem.* ...	,,	(h)al-ci	3. *Fem.* ... ,, ,,		lil-li-cu, li-li-ca
3. *Masc.* ...	,,	lil-lic li-lic			

INFINITIVE.		PARTICIPLE.	
𒆷 𒆖	la-cu	𒀠𒇷𒆖	(h) al- li - cu
		𒀀𒇷𒆖	(h)a-li-cu

PARADIGM OF THE OTHER CONJUGATIONS.

	PERMANSIVE.	PRESENT.			AORIST.		
Iphteal ...		𒀸 𒁁 𒈮		i-tal-lac	𒀸 𒁁 𒈗		i-tal-lic
„ ...		𒇷 𒈨 𒈮		it-ta-lac	„	„	it-ta-lic
Niphal ...	[nal-luc]	„	„	i-na-al-lac	„	„	i-na-al-lic
Ittaphal ...		„	„	it-tal-lac	„	„	it-tal-lic
Pael ...	al-lac	„	„	yu-'al-lac	„	„	yu-'al-lic
„ ...	„	„	„	yul-lac	„	„	yul-lic
Iphtaal ...		„	„	yu-tal-lac	„	„	yu-tal-lic
Shaphel ...	[sal-lac]	„	„	yu-sal-lac	„	„	yu-sal-lic
Istaphel ...		„	„	yus-tal-lac	„	„	yus-tal-lic

	IMPERATIVE.	PARTICIPLE.		
Iphteal ...	[it-lic]			mu-tal-la-cu
Niphal ...	na-al-lic	„	„	mu-na-al-li-cu
Ittaphal ...		„	„	mut-tal-li-cu
Pael ...	(h)ul-lic	„	„	mu-'al-li-cu
Iphtaal ...	[i-tal-lic]	„	„	mu-tal-li-cu
Shaphal ...	sul-lic	„	„	mu-sal-li-cu
Istaphal ...	[su-tal-lic]	„	„	mus-tal-li-cu

Verbs פ״י.

KAL.

	PERMANSIVE.	PRESENT.	AORIST.	IMPERATIVE AND PRECATIVE.
	Singular.	*Singular.*	*Singular.*	*Singular.*
1.	[u-la-da-cu]	u-lad	u-lid, "*I begat*"	lu-lid
2. *Masc.*		„ „ tu-lad	„ „ tu-lid	„ „ lid
2. *Fem.*		„ „ tu-la-di	„ „ tu-li-di	„ „ li-di
3. *Masc.* [u-lid] ...		yu-lad	yu-lid	„ „ lu-lid
3. *Fem.*		„ „ tu-lad	„ „ tu-lid	
	Plural.	*Plural.*	*Plural.*	*Plural.*
1.		„ „ nu-lad	„ „ nu-lid	
2. *Masc.*		„ „ tu-la-du	„ „ tu-li-du	„ „ li-du
2. *Fem.*		„ „ tu-la-da	„ „ tu-li-da	„ „ li-da
3. *Masc.* al-du [*fr.* אלד]		„ „ yu-la-du	„ „ yu-li-du	„ „ lu-li-du
3. *Fem.*		„ „ yu-la-da	„ „ yu-li-da	„ „ lu-li-da
	Dual	*Dual.*	*Dual.*	
3.		„ „ [yu-la-da-a]	„ „ [yulidā]	

INFINITIVE.	PARTICIPLE.
a-la-du	u-li-du
lā-du	a-li-du.

PARADIGM OF THE OTHER CONJUGATIONS.

	PERMANSIVE.	PRESENT.	AORIST.
Iphteal ...	[telud]	i-tu-lad	i-tu-lid
Niphal ...	[nulud]	„ „ [i-ne-lad]	„ „ [i-ne-lid]
Ittaphal ...		„ „ i-tu-lad	„ „ it-tu-lid
Pael ...	[ullad]	„ „ { yu-'ul-lad / yul-lad }	„ „ { yu-'ul-lid / yul-lid }
Iphtaal ...		„ „ yu-tul-lad	„ „ yu-tul-lid
Shaphel ...	[sulad]	„ „ yu-se-lad	„ „ yu-se-lid
Istaphal ...	[sutelad]	„ „ yus-te-lad	„ „ yus-te lid

IMPERATIVE.		PARTICIPLE.	
Iphteal	...		mu-ta-li-du
Niphal	... nu-lid	,, ,,	mu-ne-li-du
Ittaphal	...	,, ,,	mut-te-li-du
Pael	... ul-lid	,, ,,	mul-li-du, mu-li-du
Iphtaal	...	𒀀 𒁀 𒈾 𒁕 𒁕	mut-te-el-la-du
Shaphel	... su-lid	,, ,,	mu-sa-li-du, mus-te-li-du
Istaphal	... [su-te-lid]	𒈿 𒋾 𒇷 𒁕	mus-te-li-du

Verbs י״פ.

KAL.

PERMANSIVE.	PRESENT.	AORIST.	IMPERATIVE AND PRECATIVE.
Singular.	*Singular.*	*Singular.*	*Singular.*
1. [inikacu]	𒌋𒌋 𒁹 𒆷 i-na-ak	𒌋𒌋 𒋃 𒉌 i-ni-ik "*I suckled*"	𒆷 𒉌 li-nik
2. *Masc.* …	„ „ ti-na-ak	„ „ ti-ni-ik	„ „ nik
2. *Fem.* …	„ „ ti-na-ki	„ „ ti-ni-ki	„ „ ni-ki
3. *Masc.* …	„ „ i-nak	„ „ i-nik	„ „ li-nik
3. *Fem.* …	„ „ ti-nak	„ „ ti-nik	…
Plural.	*Plural.*	*Plural.*	*Plural.*
1. … …	„ „ ni-nak	„ „ ni-nik	…
2. *Masc.* …	„ „ ti-na-ku	„ „ ti-ni-ku	„ „ ni-ku
2. *Fem.* …	„ „ ti-na-ka	„ „ ti-ni-ka	„ „ ni-ka
3. *Masc.* [iniku]	„ „ i-na-ku	„ „ i-ni-ku	„ „ li-ni-ku
3. *Fem.* …	„ „ i-na-ka	„ „ i-ni-ka	„ „ li-ni-ka

PARTICIPLE.

𒌋𒌋 𒋃 𒁁 i-ni-ku

PARADIGM OF THE OTHER CONJUGATIONS.

	PERMANSIVE.	PRESENT.		AORIST.	
Iphteal	… [tenuk]	𒌋𒌋 𒀸 𒁹 𒁁 i-ti-na-ak		𒌋𒌋 𒀸 𒉌 i-ti-nik	
Niphal	… [nenuk]	„ „ i-ni-na-ak		„ „ i-ni-nik	
Ittaphal	…	„ „ it-ti-nak		„ „ it-ti-nik	
Pael	… [ennak]	„ „ i-en-nak		„ „ i-en-nik	
		„ „ in-nak		„ „ in-nik	
Iphtaal	…	„ „ yut-te-en-nak		„ „ yut-te-en-nik	
.*Shaphel*	… [senak]	„ „ yu-se-nak		„ „ yu-se-nik	
Istaphal	… [satenak]	„ „ yus-te-nak		„ „ yus-te-nik	
Istataphal	… [satetinak]	𒌋𒌋 𒀀 𒀀 𒁹 𒀀𒀀 yus-te-te-nak		„ „ yus-te-te-nik	

IMPERATIVE.			PARTICIPLE.		
Iphteal	...	[it-nik] ...			mu-ti-ni-ku
Niphal	...	ni-nik ...	,,	,,	mu-ni-ni-ku
Ittaphal	...	[ni-ti-nik] ...	,,	,,	mu-te-ni-ku
Pael	...	un-nik ...	,,	,,	mu-en-ni-ku
Iphtaal	...	it-tin-nik ...	,,	,,	mut-te-en-ni-ku
Shaphel	...	su-nik ...	,,	,,	mu-se-ni-ku
Istaphal	...	su-te-nik ...	,,	,,	mus-te-ni-ku
Istataphal	...	[su-te-te-nik]	,,	,,	[mus-te-te-ni-ku]

N.B.—All these verbs are greatly confounded with one another, and had also a tendency to adopt forms borrowed from verbs פ״ע, consequently the same verb (e.g. *asabu*) might have some forms which presupposed a verb פ״א, others which presupposed a verb פ״י (*usabu*), others which presupposed a verb פ״נ (*nasabu*), &c. Thus the precative *lusib, lusibu* given above comes not from *asabu* (verb פ״א), but from *usabu* (verb פ״י).

Verbs ע״פּ:—

KAL.

	PERMANSIVE.		PRESENT.	
	Singular.		*Singular.*	
1. ...	[epsacu]	𒀭...	e-pa-as, ep-pas	*" I make"*
2. *Masc.* ...	[epsat]	𒀭...	te-pa-as, &c.	
2. *Fem.* ...	—	„　„	te-pa-si	
3. *Masc.* ...	e-pis	„　„	e-pa-as	
3. *Fem.* ...	—	„　„	te-pa-as	
	Plural.		*Plural.*	
1. ...	—	𒀭...	ne-pa-as	
2. *Masc.* ...	—	„　„	te-pa-su	
2. *Fem.* ...	—	„　„	te-pa-sa	
3. *Masc.* ...	[e-pi-su]	„　„	e-pa-su	
3. *Fem.* ... 𒀭...	e-pi-sa	,.　„	e-pa-sa	
	Dual.		*Dual.*	
3.	[episā]	„　„	[epasā]	

	AORIST.			IMPERATIVE AND PRECATIVE.	
	Singular.			*Singular.*	
1. ... 𒀭...	e-pus	𒀭...	e-mid *" I stood"*	𒀭... li-pus	
2. *Masc.* ...	„　„ te-pus	„	te-mid	„　„ e-pus	
2. *Fem.* ...	„　„ te-pu-si	„	te-mi-di	„　„ e-pu-si	
3. *Masc.* ...	„　„ e-pus	„	e-mid	„　„ li-pus	
3. *Fem.* ...	„　„ te-pus	„	te-mid	„　„ —	
	Plural.			*Plural.*	
1. ...	„　„ ne-pus	„	ne-mid	„　„ —	
2. *Masc.* ...	„　„ te-pu-su	„	te-mi-du	„　„ e-pu-su	
2. *Fem.* ...	„　„ te-pu-sa .	„	te-mi-da	„　„ e-pu-sa	
3. *Masc.* ...	„　„ e-pu-su	„	e-mi-du	„　„ li-pu-su	
3. *Fem.* ...	„　„ e-pu-sa	„	e-mi-da	„　„ li-pu-sa	
	Dual.				
3. ...	„　„ [epusā	„	emidā]		

INFINITIVE.			PARTICIPLE.	
𒀭... e-pi-su	𒀭... a-pū-su *" to make"*		𒀭... e-pi-su	

PARADIGM OF THE OTHER CONJUGATIONS.

	PERMANSIVE.		PRESENT.		AORIST.	
Iphteal ...	𒀭𒀭𒀭 et-pus		𒀭𒀭𒀭𒀭	e-tap-pas	𒀭𒀭𒀭	e-te-pus
Niphal ...	,, ,,	[nebus]	𒀭𒀭𒀭	ip-pas, i-pas	,, ,,	ip-pis, i-pis
Ittaphal...	,, ,,	[netepus]	𒀭𒀭𒀭𒀭	it-te-pas	,, ,,	it-te-pis
Pael ...	,, ,,	[eppas]	𒀭𒀭𒀭	yup-pas	,, ,,	yup-pis
Iphtaal ...	,, ,,	—	𒀭𒀭𒀭𒀭𒀭	yu-te-ip-pas	,, ,,	yu-te-ip-pis
Shaphel ...	,, ,,	[sepas]	𒀭𒀭𒀭𒀭	yu-se-pas	,, ,,	yu-se-pis
Istaphal...	,, ,,	[satepas]	𒀭𒀭𒀭𒀭	yus-te-pas	,, ,,	yus-te-pis

	IMPERATIVE.		PARTICIPLE.	
Iphteal ...	𒀭𒀭𒀭 et-pis		𒀭𒀭𒀭	mu-te-pi-su
Niphal ...	,, ,,	ni-ip-pis	𒀭𒀭𒀭	mu-ne-pi-su
Ittaphal ...	,, ,,	ni-te-pis	𒀭𒀭𒀭	mu-te-pa-su
Pael ...	𒀭𒀭𒀭 up-pis		𒀭𒀭𒀭	mup-pi-su
Iphtaal ...	,, ,,	—	𒀭𒀭𒀭𒀭𒀭	mut-te-ip-pi-su
Shaphel ...	,, ,,	su-pis	𒀭𒀭𒀭	mu-si-pi-su
Istaphal ...	,, ,,	su-ut-te-pis	𒀭𒀭𒀭	mus-te-pi-su

The Babylonian dialect had 𒀭𒀭 *i-bus* or 𒀭𒀭𒀭 *e-i-bus, i-bas* or *e-i-bas, i-bu-su* or *e-i-bu-su*, and *i-ba-su* or *e-i-ba-su*, instead of the 3rd pers. sing. and pl. forms given above. [A Babylonian *b* often represented an Assyrian *p*.] The Babylonian dialect also said 𒀭𒀭𒀭𒀭 *yu-'ub-bas*, &c., instead of the contracted *yubbas*, &c.

CONCAVE VERBS.

KAL.

	PERMANSIVE.		PRESENT.
	Singular.		*Singular.*
1.	ca-ma-cu "*I rise*"		a-tar
	ca'-a-na-cu, "*I establish*"		at-tar "*I bring back*"
2. *Masc.*	„ „ [camat, ca'anat]		„ „ ta-tar, &c.
2. *Fem.*	—		„ „ ta-ta-ri
3. *Masc.*	ca-am		„ „ i-tar
„	ca-in		„ „ „
3. *Fem.*	„ „ [camat] [ca-i-nat]		„ „ ta-tar

	Plural.		*Plural.*
1.	— —		„ „ na-tar
2. *Masc.*	— ca-ma-tu-nu		„ „ ta-ta-ru
2. *Fem.*	— —		„ „ ta-ta-ra
3. *Masc.*	ca-mu, ca-i-nu		„ „ i-ta-ru
3. *Fem.*	„ „ ca-ma, ca-i-na		„ „ i-ta-ra

	Dual.		*Dual.*
3.	camā		„ „ i-ta-ra-a

AORIST.

	Singular.			*Plural.*		
1.	a-tur, at-tur	a-ciś "*I cut off*"		na-tur	na-ciś
2. *Masc.*	„ ta-tur, &c.	„ ta-ciś		„ ta-tu-ru	„ ta-ci-śu
2. *Fem.*	„ ta-tu-ri	„ ta-ci-śi		„ ta-tu-ra	„ ta-ci-śa
3. *Masc.*	„ i-tur	„ i-ciś		„ i-tu-ru	„ i-ci-śu
3. *Fem.*	„ ta-tur	„ ta-ciś		„ i-ta-ra	„ i-ci-śa

	Dual.		
3.	„ i-tu-ra-a	„ i-ci-śa-a

KAL.—*continued.*

IMPERATIVE AND PRECATIVE.

	Singular.		Plural.
1.	𒐊 lu-ut-tur, lu-tur-ru		
2. *Masc.*	tir, tir-ra ⟶ tar	du-ku *"smite ye;"* cinu *"establish ye"*
	cin duk	
2. *Fem.*	„ ti-ri, ta-ri, ci-ni, du-ci	„ du-cā, ci-nā
3. *M. and F.*	„ lit-tur, li-tur	„ lit-tu-ru, li-tu-ru
		Dual.
		„ lit-tu-ra, li-tu-ra

INFINITIVE.

ta'-a-ru *to turn*

PARTICIPLE ACT.

ta'-i-ru   ca'-i-nu

PARTICIPLE PASS.

ti-ru   di-ku   ci-nu

PARADIGM OF THE OTHER CONJUGATIONS.

	PERMANSIVE.			PRESENT.	
Iphteal.		{ te-bā-cu *"I come"*		ic-ta-an	
		[te-cin]		it-ba-a	
Niphalel ...	„	„	[na-ac-nu-un]	„	„ ic-ca-na-an
Ittaphalel ...	„	„	[na-ac-te-nun]	„	„ it-tac-na-an
Pael ...		ci-i-in		„	„ { yu-uc-ca-an
					yuc-ca-an
Iphtael ...	„	„	—	„	„ yuc-ta-an
Palel ...		cu-un-nu, *3rd pl.*		„	„ yuc-na-an
Iphtalel ...	„	„	—	„	„ ic-te-na-an
Shaphel ...	„	„	[sa-ca-in]	„	„ yu-sa-ca-an
Istaphal ...	„	„	[sa-te-ca-an]	„	„ yus-ta-ca-an
Aphel ...	„	„	—	„	„ yu-ca-(y)an
Itaphal ...	„	„	—	„	„ yuc-ca-an
Shaphael ...	„	„	[saccen]	„	„ yu-sac-ca-an
Istaphael ...	„	„	—	„	„ yus-tac-ca-an
Shaphel Pass.	„	„	[su-cu-un]		yu-su-ca-an

PARADIGM OF THE OTHER CONJUGATIONS.

		AORIST.		IMPERATIVE.	PARTICIPLE	
Iphteal	...	𒈨𒌋𒐊𒈨 ic-ti-in 𒈨𒌋 it-bu'	[ci-tu-un] [te-bu]	𒈨𒌋𒐊𒈨 mu-uc-ti-nu		
Niphalel	...	,, ,,	ic-ca-nin iz-za-nun	na-ac-nin	,, ,,	mu-uc-ca-ni-nu
Ittaphalel	...	,, ,,	it-tac-nin	ni-tac-nin	,, ,,	mut-tac-na-nu
Pael	...	,, ,,	yu-uc-cin yuc-cin	[uc-cin]	,, ,,	mu-uc-ci-nu
Iphteal	...	,, ,,	yuc-ti-in	—	,, ,,	mu-tac-ci-nu
Palel	...	,, ,,	yuc-ni-in	uc-ni-in	,, ,,	mu-uc-ti-nu
Iphtalel	...	,, ,,	ic-te-nin	—	,, ,,	—
Shaphel	...	,, ,,	yu-sa-cin	su-cu-un	,, ,,	mu-sa-ci-nu
Istaphel	...	,, ,,	yus-ta-cin	su-ut-cu-un	,, ,,	mu-sac-ci-nu
Aphel	...	,, ,,	yu-cin	cin, cu-un	,, ,,	mu-ci-nu
Itaphal	...	,, ,,	yuc-cin	—	,, ,,	mu-uc-ci-nu
Shaphael	...	,, ,,	yu-sac-cin	su-uc-cu-un	,, ,,	mu-sac-ci-nu
Istaphael	...	,, ,,	[yus-tac-cin]	—	,, ,,	mus-tac-ci-nu
Shaphel Pass.		𒈨𒌋𒐊𒈨 yu-su-cin		—	,, ,,	—

It will be noticed that Palel and Iphtalel regularly appear in these Concave Verbs, and that Niphalel and Ittaphalel take the place of Niphal and Ittaphal.

The permansive of Pael changes *ayya* into *i*, and has a passive or neuter signification.

Verbs ל״א, ל״ה, ל״ו, ל״י, ל״ע.

KAL.

PERMANSIVE (*or* Perfect).	PRESENT.	AORIST.
Singular.	*Singular.*	*Singular.*
1. 𒈾 na-sa-cu "*I lift up*"	𒀀 a-gab-bi' "*I speak*"	𒀝 ag-bi' 𒀊 ab-nu' "*I built*"
2. *Masc.* 𒈾 na-sa-at ...	„ „ ta-gab-bi'...	„ tag-bi' „ tab-nu
2. *Fem.* — — ...	„ „ ta-gab-bi'	„ tag-bi' „ tab-nu
3. *Masc.* 𒈾 na-su ...	„ „ i-gab-bi',i-lik-ku'	„ ig-bi' „ ib-nu'
3. *Fem.* 𒈾 na-sat ...	„ „ ta-gab-bi'	„ tag-bi' „ tab-nu'
Plural.	*Plural.*	*Plural.*
1. — — ...	„ „ na-gab-bi'	„ nag-bi' „ nab-nu,nikh-dhu
2. *Masc.* — — ...	„ „ ta-gab-bu	„ tag-bu „ tab-nu
2. *Fem.* — — ...	„ „ ta-gab-ba	„ tag-ba „ tab-na
3. *Masc.* 𒈾 na-su-u ...	„ ., i-gab-bu ...	„ ig-bu „ ib-nu
3. *Fem.* 𒈾 na-sa-a ...	„ „ i-gab-ba ...	„ ig-ba „ ib-na
Dual.	*Dual.*	*Dual.*
3. 𒈾 na-sa-a ...	„ „ i-gab-ba-a	„ ig-ba-a „ ib-na-a

IMPERATIVE AND PRECATIVE.		INFINITIVE.
Singular.		𒃻 ba-nu " *to build*"
1. 𒇻 lu-ug-bi' 𒇻 lu-ub-nu'		𒂵 ga-a-bu " *to speak*"
2. *Masc.* „ „ ba-ni, ba-an „ „ khi-dhi'		𒈾 na-a-su "*to lift*"
2. *Fem.* „ „ ba-ni-i „ „ khi-dhi-i		
3. *Masc.* „ „ li-ig-bi' „ „ li-ib-nu'		PARTICIPLE.
Plural.		𒃻 ba-nu
2. *Masc.* „ „ ba-nu-u		𒂵 ga-bu
2. *Fem.* „ ,, ba-na-a		
3. *Masc.* „ „ li-ib-nu-u		
3. *Fem.* „ „ lib-na-a		

Verbs ל״ע properly have *e* in the last syllable, as ⬠𒁹 𒑊 ⬠𒑊 *is-me-e* "he heard," but *i* frequently takes its place. In the plural we may have ⬠𒁹 𒑊 𒀹 *is-me-u* as well as ⬠𒁹 𒀹 *is-mu*.

PARADIGM OF THE OTHER CONJUGATIONS.

	PERMANSIVE.		PRESENT.
Iphteal ...	...	[kitbu']	ik-te-ba'
Pael ...	...	[kabba']	,, ,, yu-kab-ba'
Iphtaal ...	...	—	,, ,, yuk-tab-ba'
Niphal ...	nak-bu'		,, ,, ik-ka-ba'
Ittaphal ...	,, ,,	[nak-te-bu']	,, ,, it-tak-ba'
Niphael ...	,, ,,	[nakabbu']	,, ,, it-kab-ba'
Shaphel ...	,, ,,	[sakba']	,, ,, yu-sak-ba'
Istaphal ...	,, ,,	[satkeba']	,, ,, yus-te-ik-ba'
Shaphael ...	,, ,,	[sakabba']	,, ,, yus-kab-ba'
Istaphael ...	,, ,,	[satkabba']	,, ,, yus-kab-ba'
Pael Pass. ...	ku-ub-bu'		,, ,, yu-ku-ub-ba'

	AORIST.		IMPERATIVE.
Iphteal ...	ik-te-bi'		kit-bi'
Pael ...	,, ,,	yu-kab-bi'	,, ,, ku-ub-bi'
Iphtaal ...	,, ,,	yuk-tab-bi'	,, ,, ki-tib-bi'
Niphal ...	,, ,,	ik-ka-bi'	,, ,, nak-bi'
Ittaphal ...	,, ,,	it-tak-bi'	,, ,, ni-tak-bi'
Niphael ...	,, ,,	ik-kab-bi'	,, ,, [na-kab-bi']
Shaphel ...	,, ,,	yu-sak-bi'	,, ,, suk-bu'
Istaphal ...	,, ,,	yus-te-ik-bi'	,, ,, su-te-ik-bi'
Shaphael ...	,, ,,	yus-kab-bi'	,, ,, [su-ku-ub-bu']
Istaphael ...	,, ,,	yus-kab-bi'	,, ,, [su-te-ku-ub-bi']
Shaphel Pass ...	,, ,,	yu-ku-ub-bi'	—

PARTICIPLE.

Iphteal ...	muk-te-bu-u	*Niphael* ...	muk-kab-bu-u
Pael ...	,, ,, mu-kab-bu-u	*Shaphel* ...	,, ,, mu-sak-bu-u
Iphtaal ...	,, ,, muk-tab-bu-u	*Istaphal* ...	,, ,, mus-te-ik-bu-u
Niphal ...	,, ,, muk-ka-bu-u	*Shaphael* ...	,, ,, mus-kab-bu-u
Ittaphal ...	,, ,, mut-tak-bu-u	*Istaphael* ...	,, ,, mus-te-kab-bu-u

By combining the forms given in these Paradigms the student will be able to obtain the forms of *doubly defective Verbs* like 𒀀𒁀 *atsu* "to go forth," 𒀀𒁀 *lavu* "to cling to," 𒀀𒁀 *bavu* "to come."

PARADIGM OF QUADRILITERAL VERBS.

The Characters to be added by the Student.

	PERMANSIVE.				PRESENT.
Kal (=*Palel*) ...	𒀀𒁀	pal-cit			{ i-pal-cat "*he crosses*" { iś-khu-par "*he overthrows*" }
Iphtalel ...	,,	,,	[pitlucut]	𒀀𒁀	yup-tal-cat
Saphalel ...	,,	,,	[saplacat]	,,	,,	yus-pal-cat
Istaphalel ...	,,	,,	[saptelcat]	,,	,,	yus-ta-pal-cat
Niphalel ...	,,	,,	[naplacut]	,,	,,	ip-pal-cat
Ittaphalel ...	,,	,,	[naptelcut]	,,	,,	it-ta-pal-cat
Niphalla ...	,,	,,	—	,,	,,	ip-pal-ca-ta-at

	AORIST.	IMPERATIVE.	PARTICIPLE.
Kal (=*Palel*)	{ i-pal-cit, i-pa-la-cit } { ip-la-cit, iś-khu-pir }	pal-cit	mu-pal-ci-tu
Iphtalel ...	yup-tal-cit	pi-tal-cat	mu-up-tal-ci-tu
Saphalel ...	yus-pal-cit	su-pal-cut	mu-pal-ci-tu
Istaphalel ...	yus-ta-pal-cit	sit-pal-cut	mus-ta-pal-ci-tu
Niphalel ...	{ ip-pal-cit { ip-par-sud "*he pur-sued*" }	ni-pal-cat	mu-up-pal-ci-tu
Ittaphalel ...	it-ta-pal-cit	[na-te-pal-cat]	mut-ta-pal-ci-tu
Niphalla ... 𒀀𒁀	ip-pal-cit-it	... ...	mu-up-pal-cit-tu

VERBS TO BE CONJUGATED BY THE STUDENT.

1.	ca-sa-du	to obtain	21.		to extend
2.	na-ba-lu	to fall, destroy	22.		to proclaim
3.	pa-ra-tsu	to speak falsely	23.		to cut off
4.	tsa-ba-tu	to take	24.		to slay
5.	sa-dha-ru	to write	25.		to oversee
6.	sa-pa-ru	to send	26.		to make bricks
7.	ma'-a-tu	to die	27.		to thresh
8.	sa-la-dhu	to rule	28.		to measure
9.	ba-kha-ru	to choose	29.		to pour
10.	na-ca-ru	to be strange			

Verbs to be transliterated and conjugated by the Student.

Verbs to be conjugated and the Characters added by the Student.

11.		to protect	30.	ca-ra-bu	to be near
12.		to complete	31.	ka-a-su	to snare
13.		to collect	32.	e-bi-lu	to be lord
14.		to finish	33.	ha-pa-cu	to smite
15.		to hear	34.	ma-la-cu	to rule
16.		to trust	35.	ca-na-su	to submit
17.		to destroy	36.	ma-kha-ru	to be present, to receive
18.		to cross over	37.	sa-ra-cu	to deliver
19.		to curse	38.	na-du-u	to place
20.		to ask	39.	za-ca-ru	to remember
			40.	a-ba-lu	to bring

VERBS *to be conjugated and the Characters added by the Student.*

41.		e-ri-bu ...	*to descend*	59.	e-zi-bu ...	*to forsake*
42.		e-lu-u ...	*to ascend*	60.	pa-ta khu	*to cut open*
43.		e-ci-mu ...	*to strip, to take*	61.	ga-ru-u ...	*to war*
44.		sa-la-lu ...	*to spoil*	62.	sa-ca-ru...	*to drink*
45.		khar-pa-su	*to be violent*	63.	ra-tsa-pu	*to build*
46.		ca-vu-u ...	*to burn*	64.		*to build*
47.		sa-tu-u ...	*to drink*	65.		*to go*
48.		sa-la-pu...	*to pull out*	66.		*to hate*
49.		ka-lu-u ...	*to burn*	67.		*to see*
50.		na-ca-ru	*to dig*	68.		*to fill*
51.		ma-lu-u ...	*to fill*	69.		*to die*
52.		śa-kha-ru	*to go round*	70.		*to assemble*
53.		e-ni-khu	*to decay*	71.		*to burn*
54.		pa-ra-ru	*to crush*	72.		*to learn*
55.		kha-ba-tu	*to devastate*	73.		*to make*
56.		par-sa-du	*to fly*	74.		*to conquer*
57.		ta-ra-tsu	*to arrange*	75.		*to be good*
58.		na-pa-ra-cu	*to break*			

LIST OF ASSYRIAN PREPOSITIONS.

1.	𒅀 𒌋𒁉	a-di ...	*up to*	18.	im ...	*from, with*
2.	𒅀	a-khi, a-kha-at	*at the side of*	19.	ina, in ...	*in, by, with*
3.	𒅀	a-khar ...	*behind*	20.	in-na, in-nannu	*in, from*
4.	𒅀	a-na, an	*to, for*	21.	it-ti, it ...	*with, during*
5.		ar-cu, ar-ci	*after*	22.	ci ...	*according to, as*
6.		as-su, as-sum	*in, by, in regard to*	23.	ci-ma, cim	*like*
7.		ba-lu, baliv	*without*	24.	ci-bit ...	*by command of*
8.		bi-rid ...	*within, near*	25.	ci-rib ...	*in the midst of*
9.		di-khi ...	*opposite*	26.	cu-um ...	*instead of*
10.		ul-li ...	*among*	27.	la-pa-ni...	*before*
11.		ul-lā-nu	*before*	28.	li-me-ti, li	*near*
12.		ul-la-num-ma	*upon*	29.	lib-bi, libba	*in the midst of*
13.		ul-tu ...	*from, out of*	30.	makh-ri	*before*
14.		is-tu ...	*from, out of*	31.	mi-ikh-rit	*among*
15.		il-la-mu...	*before*	32.	nir ...	*below, near, against*
16.		il-la-an [or elan]	*beyond*	33.	ne-mi-du	*towards*
17.		il-lu ...	*upon*	34.	śi-khar-ti	*throughout*
				35.	e-la ...	*over*

ASSYRIAN PREPOSITIONS—*continued.*

36.	e-la-at ...	*except*	41.	pa-ni, pan	*before*
37.	e-li, el ...	*over, upon, above, beside*	42.	tsir ...	*against, upon*
			43.	sa ...	*of, in regard to*
38.	e-la-an ...	*beyond*	44.	sap-tu ...	*by the help of*
39.	e-ma ...	*around*	45.	se-pu ...	*under*
40.	er-ti ...	*against*	46.	tic ...	*behind*

THE COMPOUND PREPOSITIONS.

1.	𒀀𒈾𒀉𒋾	a-na it-ti	*to be with*
2.	𒀀𒈾𒆷	a-na la	*not to be*
3.	𒀀𒈾𒅎	a-na im	*to*
4.	𒀀𒈾𒂊�li	a-na e-li	*over*
5.	𒀀𒈾𒍇	a-na er-ti	*to the presence of*
6.		ul-tu ci-rib	*from the midst of*
7.		ul-tu lib-bi	*from the midst of*
8.		ul-tu pa-ni	*from before*
9.		i-na bi-bil, i-na bi-ib-lat	*in the midst of*
10.		i-na a-di dhe-mi	*by command of*
11.		i-na ci-rib	*in the midst of*
12.		i-na lib-bi	*in the midst of*
13.		i-na śu-ki	*in front of*
14.		i-na ni-rib	*near to*
15.		i-na la	*for want of*
16.		i-na pan	*from before*
17.		i-na e-li	*above*
18.		i-na er-ti	*after*
19.		i-na tir-tsi, i-na tar-tsi	*in the* $\left\{ \begin{array}{c} presence \\ time \end{array} \right\}$ *of*
20.		i-na an-ni	*at this time*
21.		ci la	*without*
		&c., &c.	

THE CONJUNCTIONS.

1. 𒀭 or 𒀭𒐊𒂷	u or vā	*and* (between nouns and clauses)	
𒂖	vă ...	*and* (after verbs)	
2. 𒀭, 𒂖𒐖𒌋	û ...	*or*	
3. 𒐊𒐊	ai ...	*not* (with the Imperat. or Precat.)	
4. 𒂷𒌋	ac-ca	*how?*	
5. 𒀸𒌋	im ...	*if*	
6. 𒀸𒂖	as-su	*when, meanwhile, now*	
7. 𒂖𒄑	i-nu...	*behold, now*	
8. 𒀭𒌋	cī ...	*when, thus, as, while*	
9. 𒀭𒌋𒂖	ci-ma	*as, thus*	
10. 𒂖	lā ...	*not*	
𒀭𒄑	ul ...	*not* (with verbs)	
11. 𒌋	lū ...	*whether, or, truly* (verbal prefix of past time)	

12. 𒂖 𒐊	ma-a ...	*that, for* umma (see Adverbs)	
13. 𒀵	sa ...	*when, because, where, that*	
14. 𒄑 𒂖	sum-ma	*if, thus, when*	
15. 𒀭𒌋 𒀭𒂖 𒀵	al-la sa	*after that*	
16. 𒐊 𒀭𒄑 𒀵	a-di-sa, a-di e-li sa	*in so far as, while*	
17. 𒀭𒀸𒐊𒀭 𒀭𒂖 𒀵	ar-ci sa	*after that*	
18. 𒀸𒌋 𒂖 𒀭𒐊 𒂖	im ma-ti-ma	*if at all*	
19. 𒀸 𒂖 𒀭𒐊 𒂖	i-na ma-ti-ma	*in any case*	
20. 𒀭𒂖 𒀵	ci-sa ...	*whenever*	
21. 𒂖𒐖𒄑𒀵	lib-bu sa	*just as*	
22. 𒀵 𒂖 𒀭𒐊 𒂖	sa ma-ti-ma	*of what place?*	
23. 𒂖𒐊 𒂷𒌋 𒐊𒂖	e-cā-ma	*why?*	
24. 𒀭𒄑𒄑𒄑	mi-i-nu	*how?*	

THE ADVERBS.

The most common mode of forming the adverb in Assyrian was by attaching the termination *-is* to the construct-state of a noun (whether sing. or pl.) ; as *rab-is* "greatly," *el-is* "above," *sallat-is* "for a spoil," *caccab-is* "like a star," *sadan-is* "like mountains." The accusative case of the noun, with or without the mimmation, might also be used adverbially, as *palcā* "amply," *rubam* "greatly."

The genitive also, with or without the mimmation, is sometimes found ; as *batstsi* "in ruin," *labirim* "of old."

The most common adverbs of place and time are the following :—

1.	a-gan-na ...	*here*	11.	ci-ha-am ...	*thus*
2.	a-di ...	*till*	12.	lu-ma(h)-du	*much*
3.	ai-um-ma, ya-um-ma, um-ma	*never*	13.	makh-ri ...	*formerly*
			14.	ma-te-ma...	*in times past*
	.... la		15.	e-nin-na ...	*again*
4.	al-lu, al-la, al-la sa	*then, after-wards*	16.	e-nu-va ...	*when, at that time*
5.	ar-ci ...	*afterwards*	17.	pa-na-ma...	*formerly*
6.	u-di-na ...	*at the same [time]*	18.	tsa-tis ...	*in future*
			19.	sa... ...	*when*
7.	um-ma ...	*thus, that*	20.	sa-num-ma, sa-nam-ma	*in a foreign land, else-where*
8.	ul-lā-na, ultu ulla	*from that time, from of old*			
			21.	ina yumi suma	*at that time*
9.	zi-is ...	*as of old*	22.	um-maas-su	*because*
10.	ca-la-ma ...	*of all kinds*	23.	a-di ma-ti...	*how long?*

DERIVATION OF NOUNS.

A large proportion of Assyrian nouns are derived from different forms of the verb. Thus from Kal we have the infinitives 𒀭𒀭𒀭𒀭𒀭 *ra-kha-a-tsu* "to inundate," 𒀭𒀭𒀭𒀭 *ni-ci-i-śu* "to cut off," and 𒀭𒀭𒀭𒀭 *su-mu-u-ru* "to keep;" the participle passive 𒀭𒀭𒀭𒀭 *da-li-i-khu* "troubled," and the active participle 𒀭𒀭𒀭𒀭 *ma-a-li-cu* "ruling" where the long *ā* of the first syllable serves to distinguish it from *mă-li-cu* "a king," which is derived from the Permansive.

From Pael we have nouns like 𒀭𒀭𒀭 *kar-ra-du* "war-like," *lim-mu-nu* "injured."

From Palel, 𒀭𒀭𒀭 *nam-ri-ri* "bright."

From Iphteal and Iphtaal, 𒀭𒀭𒀭 *cit-ru-bu* "a meeting," *lat-bu-su* "clothed," *git-ma-lu* "a benefactor."

From Shaphel, 𒀭𒀭𒀭 *sap-sa-ku* "an opening," *sum-cu-tu* "a slaughter."

From Niphal, 𒀭𒀭𒀭 *nab-kha-ru* "collected," *nab-ni-tu* "offspring," *num-kha-ru* "a receipt."

From the weak verbs come words like 𒀭𒀭 *mi-ru* "offspring" for *ma'-iru, sa-hu* "summit" from *nasu*, and from verbs י"פ, *lit-tu* (for *lid-tu*), *li-du*, *li-i-tu*, *li-da-a-tu*, and *lit-tu-tu*, all meaning "offspring." Also forms which repeat the second radical, as *li-lic-cu* "a going," *lil-li-du* "a birth," *dadmu* "man," the Heb. *adam* אדם.

When a monosyllable is repeated the last consonant of the first syllable is generally assimilated to the first consonant of the second syllable, as 𒀭𒀭𒀭 *kak-ka-du* (for *kad-kadu*) "a head," *ca-ac-ca-bu* (for *cab-cabu*) "a star."

The prefix *M* denotes the instrument, action, or place, as 𒀭𒀭𒀭 *man-za-zu* a "bulwark."

The prefix *T* (another form of Iphteal) builds abstracts, as 𒀭𒀭𒀭 *tas-me-a-tu* "a hearing," *te-ni-se-tu* "mankind," *tu-ku-ma-tu* or *tuk-ma-tu* "opposition." Also adjectives as *Tas-me-tu* "she who hears" (the wife of Nebo).

Roots may be increased by prefixing a vowel, as 𒀭𒀭𒀭 *al-ca-cat* or *il-ca-cat* " stories," *e-da-khu* " warrior," *im-mi-ru* " youngling," *u-ta-a-ma* " lawgiver."

A word might be lengthened by affixing *ānu* (also *īnu* or *innu* and *ūnu*) to the construct ; 𒂠𒅍 ⯈𒌋 𒅍 ⯈ *cir-ba-a-nu* " an offering," ⯈⯈ 𒂠𒅍 𒅍 ⯈ *sil-dha-a-nu* "a king," 𒄖𒅍 𒀭 𒅍 ⯈ *te-er-din-nu* "a descent," 𒅍 𒀸 ⯈ *a-gu-nu* " a crown." Words so formed were collectives.

Gentile nouns were formed by the termination *ai* (fem. *aitu*), as ⯈𒅄 𒂠 𒂠𒅍 𒅍 𒅍 *ti-(h)am-ta-ai* " a sailor," 𒄖𒄖 𒂠 𒄃 ⯈𒅍 𒅍 𒅍 *Ba-bi-la-ai* " a Babylonian," *Dur-Sar-ci-na-ai-ti* " she of Dur-Sargon."

Quadriliterals are occasionally found, as well as quinqueliterals, as *a-sa-ri-du* " first-born," *khar-pa-su* " vehemence," *kha-mi-luhk-khi* " stores," *kha-ba-tsi-il-la-tu* " a lily."

Many Assyrian words are borrowed from Accadian.

PHONOLOGY.

The chief phonetic rules to be remembered are the following :—

1. A sibilant before a dental generally becomes *l*, as *kha-mil-tu* " five " for *kha-mis-tu*.

2. A dental followed by *s* is (together with the sibilant) resolved into *śś* or *ś*, as 𒀉𒅍 𒄃𒄃 ⯈𒂠𒅍 *ka-aś-śu* or 𒀉𒅍 ⯈𒂠𒅍 *ka-śu* for *kat-su* " his hand."

3. A dental preceded by a sibilant is assimilated to the latter, and when the sibilant is *s* the last rule takes effect, as *its-tsa-bat* for *its-ta-bat* " he is taken," *iś-śa-can* and *i-śa-can* for *is-ta-can* " he dwells."

4. After a guttural, the *t* of the secondary conjugations may change to *d* or *dh*, as *ik-dha-rib* for *ik-ta-rib* " he approached."

5. *Kh* in the other Semitic idioms, is frequently replaced in Assyrian by *h*, or lost altogether.

6. Instead of *k* the Babylonian dialect often has *g*, as *ga-tu* for *ka-tu* " hand ;" and this change of letter sometimes makes its way into the Assyrian dialect.

7. *C* frequently takes the place of *k* (especially at the beginning of a word), and also (but more rarely) of *g*, as ⟨cuneiform⟩ *ci-ri-bu* for ⟨cuneiform⟩ *ki-ri-bu* " neighbourhood," ⟨cuneiform⟩ *ci-bit* for ⟨cuneiform⟩ *ki-bit* " command ;" and where the other Semitic dialects prefer the softer consonants (*g, z*), Assyrian often combines *c* and *ts* in a root.

8. *N* is generally assimilated to the following consonant, as *id-din* for *in-din* " he gave." Conversely, a double dental may be resolved into *nd* or *nt*.

9. *M* may become *n* before a dental, sibilant, or guttural, as *khan-sa* for *kham-sa* "five," and then be assimilated to the following consonant, as ⟨cuneiform⟩ *ikhkhar* for *imkhar* "it is present." Conversely, double *b* or double *p* may be resolved into *mb* or *mp*, as *i-nam-bu'* for *i-nab-bu'* " he proclaims."

10. *E* (⟨cuneiform⟩) is always a vowel, and is very frequently used as interchangeable with *i*.

N.B.—The Assyrians had considerable difficulty in adapting the characters of a foreign (Accadian) syllabary to express the sounds of their own language. Hence in the 3rd pers. sing. of a verb, whenever the form requires a prefixed *u* (in Pael, &c.), we have to supply a *y ;* thus ⟨cuneiform⟩ must be read *yus*, not *us*, ⟨cuneiform⟩ *yu*, not *u*. Before ⟨cuneiform⟩, *h* has often to be understood, and sometimes has to be supplied (though not written) after a vowel. *M* and *v* were interchangeable in Accadian, and possibly also in Assyrian ; at all events they are interchangeable in the writing, and ⟨cuneiform⟩, e.g., must sometimes be read *ma* and sometimes *va*, ⟨cuneiform⟩ sometimes *am* and sometimes *av*. The chief drawback occasioned by the syllabary was that a final guttural may be read *g, c,* or *k*, a final dental *d, dh,* or *t*, a final labial *b* or *p*, a final sibilant *s* or *ś*, and even *z* or *ts*. Thus ⟨cuneiform⟩ may be either *tig, tic,* or *tik*. Again, ⟨cuneiform⟩ represented both *za* and *tsa*, ⟨cuneiform⟩ *da* or *dha*, ⟨cuneiform⟩ *di* or *dhi*, and ⟨cuneiform⟩ *bu* or *pu*. Only a certain number of characters contained the vowel *e*. There was no *sh* or *th*.

ACCENTUATION.

It has been noted (p. 48) that a double consonant is frequently left unmarked in Assyrian writing: on the other hand we often find a double consonant written where there is no grammatical reason for its existence. It then denotes that the accent falls on the preceding vowel. Thus ⸰ na-khal-li, "valleys," stands for *nakháli*. The double consonant in the present tense of Kal has an accentual and not a formative origin; *i-sac-cin* really represents *isácin*. In Pael, on the other hand, the double consonant is a grammatical sign.

As a general rule, the accent in Assyrian is thrown back as far as possible, falling upon the antepenult, unless the penult has a long vowel or is a closed syllable (that is, a syllable beginning and ending with a consonant). The enclitic *va*, "and," threw back the accent upon the preceding syllable, even though this had a long syllable before it; e.g., *il-li-cū-niv-va* for *illicūnĭ´-va*, "they had gone, and." So also the suffixed personal pronouns, the 2nd plural and 3rd masc. sing. excepted, as *ikh-dhu-u-nin-ni* for *ikhdhūnĭ´-ni*, "they have sinned against me;" but *uc-tan-na-su* for *uctána-su*, "I establish it." This was not the case with the suffixed demonstrative *ma;* e.g., *yátima*, "me here."

As in Ethiopic, the accent falls on the second syllable of the present tense Kal; e.g., *isácin* (see *supra*) or *i-sis-si* for *isísi* from שמע. In the Niphal of verbs ל"ה the accent fell on the penult, as *il-lak-ki'* for *illáki'*, "it was taken."

The 3rd person plural of the verb seems to have had the accent on the penult, especially if the vowel of the antepenult was weakened to *i* or *e* through assimilation to the vowel of the penult; e.g., *ip-pi-sidh-dhu* for *ippisídhu*, "they were spread out;" *itsbútu*, "they seized;" *immáru* "they were visible;" *ittanúru*, "they brought back." Quadriliterals followed the rule in the accentuation of the present Kal, thus *i-pa-lac-ɛi-tu* for *ipalácitu*, "they transgressed;" *i-pa-ras-sid*, for *iparásid*.

The plural of nouns like *náciru*, "enemy;" *nákhalu*, "valley," has the accent on the penult; e.g., *nacíri*, "enemies;" *nakháli*, "valleys" (see *supra*).

The plural is thus distinguished from the genitive singular in which the accent remains on the first syllable, leading frequently to the loss of the second syllable (e.g., *nácri* for *nácǐri*, "of an enemy;" *nákhli* for *nákhăli*, "of a valley").

Such nouns as *ci-din-nu* (for *cidínu*), "ordinance;" *a-dan-nu* (for *adánu*), "season;" *a-gur-ru* (for *agúru*), "cement;" *a-gam-mu* (for *agámu*), "pool;" *cu-dur-ru* (for *cudúru*), "landmark;" *su-lum-mu* (for *sulúmu*), "alliance;" *cits-tsil-lu* (for *citstsílu*), "royal;" *bar-zil-lu* (for *barzílu*), "iron;" have the accent on the penult.

Feminine nouns in -*ătu*, -*ĭtu*, have the accent on the antepenult. On the other hand, in the Pael participle fem., we have *mu-bal-lidh-dhat* for *muballídhat*, "she that gives life."

The possessive pronouns of the 1st, 2nd and 3rd persons, when suffixed to a noun, threw the accent back upon the preceding syllable; as *panú-ca*, "thy face;" *ramanú-su*, "himself;" *ramanú-sun*, "themselves."

The 3rd person singular of the subjective aorist (pluperfect), places the accent on the penult, as *inúkhu*, "it has rested;" *ikhúzu*, "he has possessed;" *yuctínu*, "he has established;" *yudhíbu*, "he has made good." So, too, the future *yudhábu*.

In the imperative Shaphel the accent was on the ante-penultima; e.g., *sun-ni-khi* for *súnikhi*, "cause to rest."

READING LESSONS.

Extract from the Annals of TIGLATH-PILESER I (W.A.I. XVI, col. 8, line 39) :—

(39.) 𒀭𒀭𒀭 𒀭𒀭𒀭 𒀭 𒀭𒀭 𒀭𒀭 𒀭𒀭 𒀭𒀭 𒀭𒀭   (40.) 𒀭 𒀭𒀭 𒀭𒀭 𒀭𒀭
li - ta - at   kur - di - ya   ir - nin - tu   tam - kha - ri - ya
The records   of my warriors,   the battle-shout   *of my fighting,*

𒀭𒀭𒀭 𒀭 𒀭 𒀭   (41.) 𒀭 𒀭𒀭 𒀭𒀭 𒀭 𒀭 𒀭 𒀭 𒀭 𒀭 𒀭 𒀭 𒀭
suc - nu - us   naciri   tsa - ė - ru - ut   D.P. A - sur   sa   D.P. A - nu   va
the submission of enemies   *hostile   to   Asshur,   whom   Anu   and*

𒀭 𒀭   (42.) 𒀭 𒀭 𒀭 𒀭 𒀭 𒀭 𒀭 𒀭 𒀭 𒀭
D.P. Rammânu   a - na   si - tsu - ti   is - ru - cu - u - ni
Rimmon   to   destruction   have   given,

(43.) 𒀭 𒀭 𒀭 𒀭 𒀭 𒀭 𒀭 𒀭 𒀭 𒀭 𒀭   (44.) 𒀭 𒀭 𒀭
i - na   D.P. na - ra - a - ya   va   tim - me - ni - ya   al - dhu - ur
on   my tablet   and   my foundation-stone   *I   wrote;*

𒀭 𒀭 𒀭 𒀭 𒀭 𒀭 𒀭 𒀭 𒀭   (45.) 𒀭 𒀭 𒀭
i - na   bit D.P. A - nuv   va   D.P. Rammânu   ili   rabi
in   the   temple   of   Anu   and   Rimmon,   the   gods   great,

𒀭 𒀭   (46.) 𒀭 𒀭 𒀭 𒀭 𒀭 𒀭 𒀭   (47.) 𒀭
beli - ya   a - na   tsa - at   yumi   as - cu - un   va
my lords,   for   future   days   I established;   and

𒀭 𒀭 𒀭 𒀭 𒀭 𒀭 𒀭 𒀭 𒀭 𒀭   (48.) 𒀭 𒀭 𒀭 𒀭
D.P.   na - ra - a - T   sa D.P. Sam - si D.P. Rammânu   a - bi - ya   ḋ - ni - mis
the   tablets   of   Samas-Rimmon   my father   duly

𒀭 𒀭 𒀭 𒀭 𒀭   (49.) 𒀭 𒀭 𒀭 𒀭 𒀭 𒀭 𒀭 𒀭 𒀭
ab - su - us   D.P. niki   ak - ki   a - na   as - ri - su - nu   u - tir
I cleaned :   victims   I sacrificed :   to   their places   I restored (them)

(50.) 𒀀 𒈾 — a-na — *for* — ar-cat — *future* — yumi — *days,* — a-na — *for* — YU-um — *a day* — tsa-a-te — *long hereafter,* — (51.) a-na — *for*

ma-te-ma — *whatsoever* — ruba — *prince* — ARC-u — *hereafter (reigns).* — (52.) e-nu-ma — *When* — bit — *the temple* — D.P. A-nuv — *of Anu* — va — *and*

D.P. Rammânu — *Rimmon,* — ili — *the gods* — (53.) RABU-te — *great,* — beli-ya — *my lords,* — va — *and* — śi-gur-ra-a-tu — *the towers*

54.) sa-ti-na — *these* — yu-sal-ba-ru-va — *grow old, and* — (55.) e-na-khu an-khu-śu-nu — *decay, their ruins*

lu-ud-dis — *may he renew,* — (56.) D.P. na-ra-a-TI-ya — *my tablets* — va tim-me-ni-ya — *and my foundation-stones* — (57.) ni-mes — *duly*

li-ib-su-us — *may he cleanse,* — D.P. niki — *victims* — lik-ki — *may he slay,* — (58.) a-na — *to* — as-ri-su-nu — *their places*

lu-u-tir — *may he restore,* — (59.) va — *and* — sum-su — *his name* — it-ti-ya — *with mine* — lil-dhu-ur — *may he write.*

(60.) ci-ma — *Like* — ya-ti-ma — *myself,* — D.P. A-nuv — *may Anu* — va — *and* — D.P. Rammânu — *Rimmon,* — (61.) ili — *the great* — rabi — *gods,*

i-na — *in* — dhu-ub — *soundness* — lib-bi — *of heart* — (62.) va — *and* — ca-sad — *conquest* — ir-nin-te — *in battle* — dha-bis — *bountifully*

lidh-dhar-ru-su — *keep him.* — (63.) sa — *He who* — D.P. na-ra-a-TI-ya — *my inscriptions* — va tim-me-ni-ya — *and my foundation-stones*

(64.) 𒈨𒊑𒈨𒊑𒈨   i-khab-bu-u   i-śa-pa-nu
shall conceal,   shall hide,

(65.) 𒈨𒊑𒈨𒊑   a-na me i-na-du-u
to the water shall lay,

(66.) 𒈨𒊑𒈨𒊑   i-na   isati   i-kal-lu-u
with   fire   shall burn,

(67.) 𒈨𒊑𒈨   i-na   epiri
in   dust

𒈨𒊑𒈨𒊑𒈨   i-ca-ta-mu i-na bit cummi (?)
shall cover,   in a house underground (?)

(68.) 𒈨𒊑𒈨   a-sar la-a-ma-ri
a place   not seen

𒈨𒊑𒈨𒊑   pi-si-ris i-na-ci-mu
for interpretation   shall set,

(69.) 𒈨𒊑   sum sadh-ra i-pa-si-dhu-va
the name written shall erase, and

(70.) 𒈨𒊑   sum-su i-sa-dha-ru   va   mi-lim-ma
his own name shall write;   and   an attack

(71.) 𒈨𒊑   lim-na
evil

𒈨𒊑𒈨   i-kha-śa-śa-va
shall devise, and

(72.) 𒈨𒊑𒈨𒊑   a-na   pa-an   D.P. na-ra-a-TI-ya
against   the face   of   my inscriptions

(73.) 𒈨𒊑𒈨   yu-sap-ra-cu
shall cause to break,

(74.) 𒈨𒊑𒈨   D.P. A-nu   va   D.P. Assuru ili   rabi
may Anu   and   Assur, the gods   great,

𒈨𒊑   beli-ya
my lords,

(75.) 𒈨𒊑𒈨   iz-zi-is   li-cal-mu-su-va
strongly   injure   him,   and

(76.) 𒈨𒊑𒈨𒊑   ar-ra-ta ma-ru-us-ta li-ru-ru-su
(with) a curse   grievous   may they curse him;

(77.) 𒈨𒊑   śarru-śu
his kingdom

𒈨𒊑   lis-ci-bu
may they dissipate,

(78.) 𒈨𒊑𒈨   sul   cuśśi   śar(u)-ti-su   li-śu-khu
the ascent of the throne of his kingdom   may they remove

(79.) 𒀀 𒀀 𒀀 𒀀 𒀀 [𒀀] 𒀀 𒀀
tsab - hi   bilu - ti - su   lu - bal - lu
the armies   *of his lordship*   *may they devour,*

(80.) 𒀀 𒀀 𒀀 𒀀
cacci - su
his weapons

𒀀 𒀀 𒀀 𒀀 𒀀
lu - sab - bi - ru
may they break,

(81.) 𒀀 𒀀 𒀀 𒀀 𒀀 𒀀 𒀀 𒀀 𒀀 𒀀 𒀀
a - bi - ic - ti   um - ma - ni - su   lis - cu - nu
the destruction   *of his army*   *may they cause;*

(82.) 𒀀 𒀀 𒀀 𒀀 𒀀 𒀀 𒀀 𒀀 𒀀
i - na   pa - an   naciri - su   ca - mis
in the   *presence*   *of his enemies*   *wholly*

(83.) 𒀀 𒀀 𒀀 𒀀 𒀀
lu - se - si - bu - su
may they cause him to dwell;

𒀀 𒀀 𒀀 𒀀 𒀀
D.P. Rammânu i - na   śimmi
may the Air-god with   *pestilence*

(84.) 𒀀 𒀀 𒀀 𒀀 𒀀 𒀀 𒀀
khul - te mat - śu   li - ib - tsu
destructive his land   *cut off;*

(85.) 𒀀 𒀀 𒀀 𒀀 𒀀 𒀀 𒀀 𒀀
śu - un - ka   pu - pu - ta   khu - sakh - khu
want   *of crops,*   *famine,*   (*and*)

(86.) 𒀀 𒀀 𒀀 𒀀
pagri   a - na
corpses   *against*

𒀀 𒀀 𒀀 𒀀 𒀀
mat - ti - su   lid - di'
his land   *may he lay;*

(87.) 𒀀 𒀀 𒀀 𒀀 𒀀 𒀀 𒀀 𒀀 𒀀
ana bil - ut   ma - la - a - ti - su   lik - bi'
against the sovereignty of his full-power   *may he speak;*

(88.) 𒀀 𒀀 𒀀 𒀀 𒀀 𒀀 𒀀 𒀀
sum - su   zir - su   ina mati   lu - khal - li - ik
his name,   *his seed*   *in the land*   *may he destroy.*

ANALYSIS.

39. *lītat*, pl. fem., construct form.

kurdi, for *kurădi*, pl. of *kuradu* "warrior;" perhaps Ar. قَدِير.

ya, poss. pron., first person suffix.

irnintu, with vowel prefix, from רנן "to shout for joy."

40. *tamkhari*, gen. sing., Tiphel derivative from מהר "to be present," facing;" hence "opposition" or "fighting."

sucnus, sing. construct, Shaphel passive deriv. from כנש "to subject."

náciri, masc. pl. gen., Kal participle of נכר, the Kal of which is not used in Hebrew.

41. *tsa'erut*, masc. pl., construct of the Kal part., *tsa'iru* "enemy," Heb. צר. The plural is also found under the forms *tsa'eri, tsa'iri, tsahri* and *tsayâri*. *E* is incorrectly written for *'i*, which stands for *vi*.

Anu was originally the sky, *Rimmon* was the air-god.

42. *sitsuti*, sing. gen. fem. verbal noun.   Aram. שׁצא, Targ. שׁצו "to destroy."

isrucūni, third pl. masc. perf., Kal of *saracu*.

43. *narā* (preceded by D.P. of "stone" *abnu*), apparently borrowed from Accadian. *Narā* (or *narū*) is fem., with pl. *narāti*.

timmeni, pl. masc., borrowed from Accadian.

44. *aldhur* for *asdhur*, 1st pers. sing. aor. Kal of שׁטר "to write."

bīt (for *bayit*), sing. construct; Heb. בית.

45. *ili*, pl. masc. of *'ilu*; Heb. אל.

rabi, also *rabuti*, masc. pl., adj.; Heb. רב.

bili or *beli*, pl. masc. of *belu*, Heb. בעל.

46. *tsāt*, fem. pl. construct; abstract noun from יצא (Ass. *atsu*) "to go forth" (literally "the goings forth," "that which will go forth").

yumi, pl. masc. of *yumu*, Heb. יום.

ascun, 1st pers. sing. aor. Kal of שׁכן (originally Shaphel of כן).

48. *'abi*, gen. sing. masc. of *abu* (אב).

　　'animes, adverb in *-is* formed from pl. of *'anu*, "suitably, fitly." Cp. Ar. انى

　　absus, 1st per. sing. aor. Kal of בשש "to cleanse."

　　niki, pl. of *niku* "offering," "sacrifice;" Heb. נִקָּה.

49. *akki*, 1st pers. sing. aor. Kal of נקה (*naku'u*), from which *niku* is derived.

　　'asri, pl. of *'asru*, "a place;" Aram. (& Ar.) אתר.

　　utir, 1st pers. sing. aor. Aphel of *tāru*, "to come back," become," "be;" Heb. תור "to go about."

50. *'arcāt*, pl. fem. construct of an abstract *'arcu* for *aricu*, "after" p. ארך.

　　yum tsāte literally "day of the future;" *yum* in construct sing., *tsāte* abstract fem. pl.

51. *matema* "at any time," "at any place;" Cp. Heb. מתי "when."

　　rubu, from רב, literally "a great one."

52. *enuma*, adverb compounded of *enu* (Ar. عدى عنا), and the pron. *ma* "that."

53. *sigurrātu*, pl. fem. of *sigurrătu*, "a closed place," hence "a temple-tower" or observatory, from סגר. It is written *ziggurrătu* in the Babylonian dialect.

54. *sātina*, pl. fem. of the pron. *su'atu*, *sātu*, agreeing with *sigurrātu*.

　　yusalbaru-va, 3rd pers. masc. aor. Shaphel of *labaru* "to be old," with the enclitic conjunction *va* (ו) "and."

55. *enakhu*, 3rd. pers. masc. pl. aor. Kal of ענה.

　　'ankhusunu, for *ankhut-sunu*, *t + s* being replaced not only by *t + s*, but also by *s* alone.

　　ankhut is pl. masc. from *'ankhu* a subst. derived from ענה, *'ayin* becoming *'a*.

　　luddis, 3rd sing. masc. Precative Aphel of *hadasu* "to be new." Cp. Heb. חדש.

57. *nimes* for *'animes*, as in line 48. Verbs פ"א drop their initial radical in many forms. (See my *Assyrian Grammar*, p. 108).

　　libsus, 3rd masc. sing. prec. Kal from *basasu* (as above).

　　likki', 3rd masc. sing. prec. Kal from *niku'u* (as above), the nasal being assimilated to the following letter.

58. *lutir*, 3rd masc. sing. prec. Aphel of *tāru* (as above).

59. *sum*, sing. masc. construct of *sumu* "a name;" Heb. שם.

itti, preposition; Heb. את.

lildhur, 3rd masc. sing. prec. Kal of *sadharu* (as above).

60. *yatima*, 1st pers. pron., compounded of *ya* "I," the suffix *ti*, and the pron. *ma*.

61. *dhub*, sing. construct of the subst. *dhubu*; Heb. טוב (see line 62).

libbi, gen. sing. of *libbu* "heart;" Heb לב.

62. *casad*, sing. masc. construct of *casadu* "a possession," from *casadu* "to conquer."

irninte, gen. sing. of the collective *irnintu* (as above); "possession of the battle-cry" = "victory in battle."

dhābis, adverb in -*is* from *dhabu* "good" (as in line 61). *Dhābu* is for *dhăvăbu*.

lidhdharru, 3rd pl. masc. prec. Kal of *nadharu* "to guard;" Heb. נטר.

64. *ikhabbu'u*, 3rd sing. masc. future Kal of *khabū* "to hide;" Heb. חבא. (For the form see my *Assyrian Grammar*, pp. 52, 53, 69).

isápanu for *isappanu*, 3rd sing. masc. fut. Kal of *sapanu* "to sweep away," with *a* for *i* in the 3rd syllable; Cp. Heb. ספה.

65. *me*, pl. masc. of *mu* "a drop of water." The reduplicated pl. *mami* also occurs; Heb. מים.

inádu'u for *inaddu'u*, 3rd sing. masc. fut. Kal of *nadu'u* "to place;" Cp. Ar. ند�ۤ.

66. *'isati*, pl. gen. fem. of *'isu* "fire" (Heb. אש).

ikallu'u, 3rd sing. masc. fut. Kal of קלה "to burn" (as in Heb. and Ar.)

67. *epiri*, pl. of *ipru* or *epru* "dust;" Heb. עפר.

icátumu for *icattumu*, 3rd sing. masc. fut. Kal of כתם, with *u* instead of *i* in the 3rd syllable.

bit cummi (?). Conjectural transliteration. The first ideograph is "house" (*bitu*), the second "high" or "precious" (*ellu*), and the third "god" (*'ilu*). The second and third, however, must be taken together as a compound ideograph, and perhaps denote the Assyrian Pluto.

68. *lâ amari;* *lâ* "not" (Heb. לֹא), *amari*, the gen. masc. pl. after construct *asar* of the adjective *amaru* "seen;" therefore literally "things seen" (Cp. Heb. אוּר).

pisiris, adverb, in -*is* from *pisiru* "an interpretation" (Heb. and Aram. פשר).

inácimu for *inaccimu*, 3rd sing. masc. fut. Kal of נכם "to take."

69. *ipásidhu* for *ipassidhu*, 3rd sing. masc. fut. Kal of *pasadhu* "to strip" (Heb. פשט).

70. *isadharu* for *isadhdharu* (with *a* for *i*), 3rd sing. masc. fut. Kal of *sadharu* (as above).

milimma, acc. sing. of *milimma* or *milimmu*, from לוה "to cleave to." A variant reading gives *lumima* or *luviva*, apparently from the same root.

71. *limna*, acc. sing. masc. of the adj. *limnu* (for *limunu*), agreeing with *milimma;* perhaps akin to Heb. (and Ar.) לחם "to fight."

ikhasasa-va for *ikhassasa*, 3rd sing. masc. fut. Kal of *khasasu*, with final *u* changed to -*a* through the influence of the same vowel in both the following and the preceding syllables; Cp. Æth., *khasasa* "to investigate;" Ar. *khassa.*

72. *pān*, construct of *pānu* "face;" Heb. פנים.

73. *yusapracu*, 3rd sing. masc. fut. Shaphel of פרך "to break."

75. *'izzis*, adverb in -*is*, from *'izzu* "strong;" Heb. עו.

licálmu, 3rd pl. masc. prec. Pael of כלם "to injure" or "revile," contracted from *licallĭmu.*

76. *'arrăti*, sing. fem. subst., from ארר "to curse" (see *liruru* below).

marusta for *marutsta*, fem. adj., agreeing with *'arrati*, from מרץ "to be violent" or "hard."

liruru, 3rd pl. masc. prec. Kal of ארר.

77. *sarrusu* for *sarrut-su; sarrut* fem. abstract sing. construct. Heb. שׂר "king."

liscibu, 3rd pl. masc. prec. Kal of *sacabu* "to pour out;" Ar. سكب

78. *sul*, construct sing. of *sūlu* "ascent;" Shaphel pass. derivative of עלה "to ascend." The ideograph may also be read *isid* "foundation" (Heb. יסוד).

cussu, construct sing. of *cussu'u* "throne" (as in Heb.)

lisukhu for *lissukhu*, 3rd pl. masc. prec. Kal of כסח "to remove."

79. *tsabhi*, pl. construct of *tsabu* (Heb. צבא) "an army."

luballu, 3rd pl. masc. prec. Pael of בלע "to devour."

80. *cacci*, pl. of *caccu* "a weapon;" perhaps for *carci* (Aram. כרך "armour ").

lusabbiru, 3rd pl. masc. prec. Pael of שבר "to break."

81. *'abicti*, fem. abstract; Cp. Heb. הפך "to destroy."

'ummani, gen. sing. fem. of *'ummanu* "army;" Cp. Heb. המון "multitude."

liscunu, 3rd pers. masc. pl. prec. Kal of *sacanu* (as above).

82. *camis*, adverb in *-is*, from *camu*; Cp. Ar. كام.

83. *lusesibu*, 3rd pers. pl. masc. prec. Shaphel of *asibu* "to dwell;" Heb. ישב.

simmi, gen. sing. masc. of *simmu* "a plague;" Cp. Heb. שמם.

84. *khulte*, adj. agreeing with *simmi*; Cp. Heb. חלה. The Semitic root seems to have been borrowed from Accadian.

mat, construct sing. of *madu* or *mātu* "country," of Accadian origin (*ma-da*); Cp. Aram. מתא. (See line 86).

libtsu, 3rd pl. masc. prec. Kal of בצע "to cut off."

85. *sunka*, acc. sing. of *sunku*; Cp. Talm. סנוק "scantiness," "frugality."

bubuta, acc. sing. of *bubutu* "crops;" perhaps Heb. ניב "fruit" may be compared. *Bubuta* is in opposition to *sunka*.

khusakhkha, acc. sing. of *khusakhkhu* "need" (Aram. חשח).

86. *pagri*, acc. pl. masc. of *pagru* "a corpse" (Heb. פגר).

matti for *madti* (or perhaps *māti*), gen. sing. of *mātu* (see line 84).

liddi,' 3rd pers. sing. masc. prec. Kal of נדה (see above).

87. *malātisu* for *malātit-su*; *malātit*, construct of abstract in ית, from *malāti*, pl. fem., from מלא "to fill."

likbi', 3rd sing. masc. prec. Kal of קבה (in Heb., "to curse ").

88. *zir*, construct sing. of *zir'u* or *zer'u* "seed" (Heb. זרע).

lukhallik, 3rd sing. masc. prec. Pael of חלק (" to divide," hence) "to scatter," "destroy."

THE LEGEND OF ISTAR.—OBVERSE.

The Cuneiform Characters to be supplied by the Student.

1. A-na   mat   NU-GA-A   kak-ka-ri   i-di-ya
   To the land of Hades,   regions of corruption,

2. D.P.   Istaru   banat   D.P.   Śini   u-zu-un-sa   [ci-nis]
   Istar,   daughter   of the Moon-god,   her attention   [determinedly]

3. is - cun - va   banat   D.P.   śini   u - zu - un - [sa   is - cun]
   fixed,   and   the daughter of the Moon-god   her attention   fixed

4.   a - na   bit   e - di - e   su - bat   'il   Ir - kal - la
   (to go) to the house of corruption,   the dwelling   of the deity Irkalla ;

5. a - na   biti   sa   e - ri - bu - su   la   a - tsu - u
   to   the house whose   entrance (is)   without exit,

6. a - na   khar - ra - ni   sa   a - lac - ta - su   la   ta - ai - rat (u)
   to   the road   whose   way (is)   without return,

7. a - na   biti   sa   e - ri - bu - su   zu - um - mu - u   nu - u - ra
   to   the house (at) whose   entrance   they bridle in   the light ;

8.   a - sar   epru   mahdu   bu - bu - uś - śu - nu   a - cal - su - nu   dhi - idh - dhu
   a place (where) dust   much   (is) their food,   their victuals   (is) mud ;

9. nu - u - ru   ul   im - ma - ru   ina   e - dhu - ti   as - bā
   (where) light   not   they see,   in   darkness   they dwell ; and

10. cal (?) - su - ma   cima   its - tsu - ri   tsu - bat   cap-pi
    ?   like   birds (is)   the erecting of (their) wings ;

11. eli   dalti   u   sac - cul - sa   mukh   ep - ru
    over   the door   and   its wainscoting   abundance   of dust.

12. D.P. Istaru   a - na   bâbi   D.P.   NU-GA-A   ina   ca - sa - di - sa
    Istar,   to (at) the gate   of Hades   at   her arrival

13. a - na   NI - GAB   ba - a - bi   a - ma - tuv   iz - zac - car
    to   the porter   of the gate   (his) duty   reminds ;

14. a - na   ni - gab   me - e   pi - ta   ba - ab - ca
    to   the porter   of the waters :   Open   thy gate !

15. pi - ta - a   ba - ab - ca - va   lu   ir - ru - ba   a - na - cu
     Open   *thy gate, and let*   *me enter in;*

16. sum - ma   la   ta - pat - ta - a   ba - a - bu   la   ir - ru - ba   a - na - cu
     if   *not* *thou openest*   *the gate (and) not*   *I enter in,*

17. a - makh - kha - ats   dal - tuv   śic - cu - ru   a - sab - bir
     I force   *the gate,*   *the bolt*   *I break,*

18. a - makh - kha - ats   śi - ip - pu   va   u - sa - pal - cit   dalâti
     I force   *the threshold, and*   *I cross*   *the doors,*

19. u - se - el - la   mi - tu - ti   acili   pal - dhu - ti
     I raise   *the dead,* *the devourers* *of the living;*

20. eli   pal - dhu - ti   i - ma - hi - du   mi - tu - ti
     above the   living   *exceed*   *the dead.*

ANALYSIS.

1. The Accadian MAD NU-GA-A is literally "land of the not returning,"
    ga'a being the participle of *gā* "to return" (see *Syllabary*). It is
    rendered in Ass. by *mat-la-naciri.* "The land from whence is no
    return" is a good name for Hades.

    kakkari, acc. pl. of *kakkaru,* Heb. כבר (see my *Assyrian Grammar*, p. 29).

    édi, written *éde* in line 4, gen. sing. of *édu* "corruption," as Dr. Schrader has
    well explained it from עדה "to pass away."

2. *Istar,* the Hebrew Ashtoreth (Astarte), the Moon-goddess and Semitic
    Venus.

    bánat, construct sing. fem. of *banatu* (also *bintu,* i.e. *binitu*) "daughter"
    (Heb. בת). Sin, the Moon-god.

    'uzun, construct sing. of *'uzunu* or *'uznu* "ear" (Heb. אזן).

    cinis ?, supplied by Dr. Schrader, adverb in *-is* from adj. *cinu* (כן).

3. *iscun,* 3rd sing. masc. aor. of *sacanu.* It will be noticed that here as
    frequently elsewhere a feminine nominative is joined to a masc. verb.

4. *subat,* construct sing. fem. of *subătu* from ישב "to sit" or "dwell."

5. *eribu*, nom. sing. masc. infinitive (or verbal noun) from ערב "to enter" or "descend."

   'atsu, nom. sing. masc. verbal noun from יצא "to go out." The literal translation of the line is "of which its entering (there is) no outgoing."

6. *khar-ra-ni*, sing. oblique case of *kharranu*, a word originally borrowed from Accadian, which gave a name to the city of Kharran or Haran (Gen. xi. 31, &c.)

   'alacta or *halacta*, sing. fem. of *halactu* from הלך "to go."

   tairat for *tairatu* (as often in the case of characters which denote syllables beginning and ending with a consonant), for *tayartu*, sing. fem. from תור "to return."

7. *zummu*, 3rd pl. masc. (used impersonally) Permansive (or Perfect) Palel of זום. Cp. Targ. זמם "bridle." In Ass. *zumani* "impassable" is used of roads.

   nura, acc. sing. of *nuru* "light" (so in Heb. [נר], Aram. and Ar.)

8. *'asar* "a place" (*see above*) often has the relative *sa* ("in which," "where") understood after it.

   mahdu, nom. sing. masc. adj. agreeing with *epru*. Cp. Heb. מאד.

   bubussunu for *bubut-sunu* (*see above*).

   'acal, construct sing. of the verbal noun *ácalu* "food," from אכל "to eat."

   dhidhdhu, nom. sing. in opposition to *acal*. Heb. טיט.

9. *immaru*, 3rd pers. pl. masc. present Kal of נמר, contracted from *inammaru*.

   edhuti, gen. sing. of *edhutu* "darkness," from עטה, "to hide," as Dr. Schrader has pointed out.

   'asbā, contracted from *asbū-a* for *asbū-va*, 3rd pl. masc. Permansive (or Perfect) Kal of *'asabu*, contracted from *'asibu* (also *yasibu*), with the enclitic conjunction.

10. The first word I cannot read.

    'itstsuri, pl. masc. of *'itstsuru* "a bird" (Ar. عصفور, Heb. צפור).

    tsubat, construct sing. fem. of *tsubātu* "a placing," from יצב. The reading and meaning of the word, however, are uncertain.

    cappi, pl. masc. of *cappu*, contracted from *canapu* (Heb. כנף), the double letter resulting from the assimilation of the nasal.

11. *dalti*, gen. sing. fem. of *daltu* (for *dalătu*) " door." (So in Heb.)

    saccul, construct sing. of *sacculu*, which Dr. Schrader has well compared with Ar. شَكل "likeness." A Syllabary makes *mescalū* a synonyme of *daltu*.

    mukh, construct sing. of *mukhkhu*, from the adjective *makh*, which was borrowed from Accadian.

12. *bâbi*, gen. sing. of *bâbu* "gate" (as in Heb., &c.)

    casidi, gen. sing. masc. of the verbal noun *casadu* "a reaching," from *casadu* " to take;" Cp. Ar. كسَد.

13. *NIGAB*, the Accadian equivalent of the Assyrian *kipu*.

    'amātuv, sing. fem. for *'amantuv* "fealty," "duty;" Heb. אמת " faithfulness."

    izzaccar, for *iztaccar*, 3rd sing. masc. present Iphteal of זכר.

14. *mē* "waters" (as above).

    pitā, for *piti-a* with the augment of motion, 2nd sing. masc. imperative Kal of *patâ* "to open;" Heb. פתח. See also next line.

15. *irruba*, 1st pers. sing. masc. aor. Kal with augment of motion, from *eribu*. The *ayin* of the first syllable is replaced by a reduplication of the 2nd radical.

16. *summa*, adverb, perhaps from שום "to place."

    tapattā, 2nd pers. sing. present Kal with augment of motion, from *patā*.

17. *amakhkhats*, 1st pers. sing. pres. Kal of מחץ.

    śiccuru, sing. noun (a pael derivative) ; Cp. Aram. סברא "bolt."

    asabbir, 1st pers. sing. pres. Kal of שבר.

18. *śippu*, sing. noun ; Heb. סף.

    usapalcit, 1st pers. sing. aor. Shaphel of the quadriliteral *palcitu* ; Cp. Ar. فلت (?)

19. *usella*, 1st pers. sing. pres. Shaphel of עלה "to ascend," with *ll* on account of the *ayin*.

    mitūti, pl. masc. part. pass. Kal of מות "to die."

    'acili, pl. construct part. pres. Kal of *acalu*, "to eat."

    paldhūti, pl. masc. part. Kal of *paladhu* or *baladhu*, "to live;" Cp. Heb. פלט.

20. *imahidu*, 3rd pers. pl. masc. pres. Kal of *mahadu* (whence *mahdu*, "much," line 7).

THE SACRIFICE OF CHILDREN (K 5139).

The transliteration to be supplied by the Student.

1. 𒁹 ... ...
   ?   may   he   remove,   and

2. ... ...
   the   offspring   who   raises   the   head   among   men,

3. ... ...
   the   offspring   for   his   life   he   gave,

4. ... ...
   the head   of   the   offspring   for   the   head   of   the   man   he   gave,

5. ... ...
   the brow   of   the   offspring   for   the   brow   of   the   man   he   gave,

6. ... ...
   the breast   of   the   offspring   for   the   breast   of   the   man   he   gave.

NOTES.

1. From נסע.

2. Cp. Ar. ورص "to bear eggs." Notice the correct use of the case-endings in this inscription.

   The Accadian SAK ILA (so *gadhu-la* is to be read), literally "head-raising," must be replaced by some corresponding Ass. adj. or part. of which -*u* is the phonetic complement. The Syllabaries render the words by *risa-nasū*.

   aveluti, abstract fem. sing.

5. *cisad* (see *casadi* above).   6. With *irtu* comp. Heb. עור "skin."

FROM THE HYMN TO SIN (K. 2861).

The English translation to be supplied by the Student.

1. bil - luv   e - bil - li   ili   sa   ina   same   u   irtsi - tiv

    e - dis - si - su   tsi - i - ru

2. a - bu   D.P. Na - an - nar   bel - luv   'ilu   dhabu   e - bil - li   ili

3. a - bu   D.P. Na - an - nar   bil - luv   i - lu   rab - u   e - bil - li   ili

4. a - bu   D.P. Na - an - nar   bil - luv   D.P. Śinu   e - bil - li   ili

5. a - bu   D.P. Na - an - nar   be - el   U - ri - e   e - bil - li   ili

6. a - bu   D.P. Na - an - nar   be - el   bit   śamulli   e - bil - li   ili

7. a - bu   D.P.   Na - an - nar   be - el   a - gi - e   su - bu - u

    e - bil   li   ili

8. a - bu   D.P. Na - an - nar   sa   śar - ru - tav   ra - bis   suc - lu - luv

    e - bil - li   ili

9. a - bu   D.P. Na - an - nar   sa   ina   ti - di - ic   ru - bu - tav

    i - nad - di - khu   e - bil - li   ili

10. 𒀭 𒀭 𒁉 𒊭 𒅀 𒂍 𒄷 𒈾 𒊩 𒀭 𒁉 𒈨 𒊑 𒋾

bú - ru   ik - du   sa   kar - ni   gab - ba - ru   sa   mes - ri - ti

suc - lu - luv   sic - ni   uc - ni - i   sac - nu

11. cu - uz - bu - u   la - la - a   ma - lu - u

NOTES.

1. *ebilli*, 3rd pers. masc. aor. (with *i* termination) "he rules," from עבל another form of בעל.

'edissi-su "he alone," anomalously formed from adverb *édis*.

tsīru, "supreme." Comp. Arabic ظهر.

2. *Nannar*, " the luminary," a name of Sin, the Moon-god.

5. *Ure*, gen. of Ur, the city of Uru (now *Mugheir*).

6. *samulli* (in Accadian SIR-GAL) = " image." Heb. סמל.

7. *age* = " of crowns "; (the Semitic root was borrowed from Accadian).

subū, Shaphel pass. part. of בוא " to come " (referring to the moon's motion).

8. *suclulu*, Shaphalel pass. part. of יכל " to be able," " to prevail."

9. *tidic*, construct sing. of a (Tiphel) noun with prefixed *t*, from *dācu* (= Heb. דכה).

inaddikhu = " he will drive."

10. *bu'-ru*, or *buhru* = " brilliance " (as in Ar.)

ikdu = " mighty " (of Accadian origin).

mesriti = " the feet " or " limbs." Dr. Schrader compares the Heb. שרין " coat of mail," which in Aram. signifies " the artery " or " nerve."

sicni = " habitations."

ucnī = " marble " (probably of Accadian origin).

11. *cuzbū* = " beauty." Norris compares Heb. קצב.

lalā = " fulness," from Accadian *lal*, " to fill " (see *Syllabary*).

Hunting Inscriptions of Assur-bani-pal (W.A.I. I, pl. 7).

The text to be transliterated by the Student.

1. 𒀭 . 𒀭 . 𒀭 . 𒀭 . 𒀭 . 𒀭 . 𒀭 . 𒀭 . 𒀭 .
    𒀭 . 𒀭 . 𒀭 .

2. 𒀭 . 𒀭 . 𒀭 . 𒀭 .
    𒀭 . 𒀭 . 𒀭 . 𒀭 . 𒀭 . 𒀭 .

3. 𒀭 . 𒀭 . 𒀭 . 𒀭 . 𒀭 . 𒀭 .
    𒀭 . 𒀭 . 𒀭 . 𒀭 . 𒀭 .

NOTES.

1.   𒀭 "the good god," became the usual designation of Assur.

    𒀭 "the lady of the abyss," or "underworld," was a title of Beltis.

    'emuci, pl. of the substantive *'emuku*, "a deep power," "a divinity" (Heb. עָמֹק).

2.   *yusatlimu's*, "they conferred on him," 3rd pl. masc. aor. Shaphel of *talamu*, with the possessive pronoun *s* contracted from *su*.

    𒀭 "great dog," was the Accadian name of "the lion" (Ass. *nesu*).

    adducu, Heb. דכה; notice the tense.

    𒀭 means "a bow," with the D.P. of *wood* and the phonetic complement *ānu*; but the reading of the word is uncertain.

    izzitu, adj.; Cp. Heb. עַז.

    𒀭 "the goddess 15," symbol of Istar.

3.   *azkup*, root זקף.

    mukhkhuru, "an offering," from מחר "to present."

    sun, contracted for *sunu*.

The text to be transliterated by the student.

1. [cuneiform text]

2. [cuneiform text]

3. [cuneiform text]

NOTES.

1. *multahti*, "renown," fem. abstract from the Iphteal part. of שאה "to make a noise," with *l* before *t* for *s*.

   issu, "fierce;" Cp. Heb. עסס (Aram. עסי) "to tread," "oppress."

2. *sa* = "of whom."

   tsir, "back" (Ar. ظهر).

   tuculti = "service."

   takhazi, weakened from *takhatsi*, for *takhkhatsi* (*tamkhatsi*) "battle," from מחץ.

3. D.P. *asmare*, "spears;" Cp. Heb. מסמר "a nail."

   aznik = "I pierced" (Cp. Heb. זק "a dart," זנק "to shoot forth"). The printed text gives *azkhul*, which must be wrong.

   zumur, "body;" ideograph of "body" or "skin," with phonetic complement *mur*. Delitzsch compares the Talmud צמורה "wind in the stomach."

The text to be transliterated by the Student.

1. 𒀭 𒈗 . 𒁹 𒈫 . 𒊩 . 𒁹 . 𒊩 . 𒀭 𒈗 .

2. 𒈨 𒁹 𒌷 𒅗 . 𒈨 𒅗 . 𒁉 . 𒅆 𒌷 . 𒍦 . 𒌷 . 𒁹 . 𒈨 . 𒉌 𒌷 . 𒀀 𒈨 . 𒁉 .

3. 𒈨 . 𒀭 𒌋 . 𒀭 𒁶 𒅆 . 𒀭 𒄄 . 𒀭 𒍑 . 𒅗 𒀀 𒊩 . 𒁉 .

4. 𒈨 . 𒁉 𒀭 𒀝 𒀀 𒅗 𒁉 . 𒌷 . 𒌷 . 𒁉 . 𒅆 𒈬 . 𒁉 . 𒌋 𒍦 𒅗 .

NOTES.

2. *melulti rubuti* "the action" or "right of sovereignty;" *melulti*, fem. abstract from עלל "to act" (especially "to act wonderfully"). Schrader reads *menarti* "might."

3. *cibit* = "command" (with weakened guttural from קבה).

   𒀭 𒁶 𒅆 = Adar.

   𒀭 𒄄   = Nergal.

ticli "ministers;" same root as *tucultu*.

4. D.P. *khutbale* = "ropes," Heb. חבל.

  mukhkha   = "brains." (See Syllabary, No. 131).

  umatti', 1st pers. aor. Pael, "I struck." Ar. ضب "to strike with a club."

From the Black Obelisk of SHALMANESER (Layard's Insc. pl. 96 l. 159.)

The text to be transliterated by the Student.

159. 𒀭 . 𒐏 . 𒈗𒈗 . 𒈗 . 𒈗 . 𒀭 . 𒈗 . 𒈗 .
𒈗𒈗𒈗𒈗 . 𒈗𒈗 .

160. 𒈗𒈗𒈗 . 𒈗 . 𒈗 . 𒈗 . 𒈗𒈗𒈗 . 𒈗 .
𒈗 . 𒈗𒈗𒈗 . 𒈗 . 𒈗 .

161. 𒈗𒈗 . 𒀭 . 𒈗 . 𒈗𒈗 . 𒈗 . 𒈗𒈗 .
𒈗𒈗 . 𒈗𒈗 . 𒈗 . 𒈗 .

162. 𒈗 . 𒈗𒈗 . 𒈗 𒈗 . 𒈗 .
𒈗𒈗 . 𒈗 . 𒈗𒈗 .

163. 𒈗 𒈗 . 𒈗 . 𒈗 . 𒈗𒈗 . 𒈗 .
𒈗 𒈗 𒈗 . 𒈗 𒈗 . 𒈗 𒈗 .

164. 𒈗 . 𒈗 . 𒈗 . 𒈗𒈗 . 𒈗 𒈗 𒈗 .
𒈗 𒈗 . 𒈗 . 𒈗 . 𒈗𒈗 . 𒈗 .

165. 𒈗 𒈗 𒈗 . 𒈗 𒈗 . 𒈗𒈗𒈗 . 𒈗 𒈗 .
𒈗 . 𒈗 . 𒈗 𒈗 . 𒈗 . 𒈗 .

166. 𒈗𒈗 . 𒈗 . 𒈗 . 𒈗𒈗 𒈗 . 𒈗 . 𒈗 . 𒀭 .
𒈗𒈗 . 𒈗 . 𒀭𒈗 . 𒈗 . 𒈗 . 𒀭 . 𒈗𒈗 .

167. 𒈗𒈗 . 𒀭 . 𒈗𒈗 𒈗 . 𒈗 . 𒀭 . 𒈗𒈗 . 𒀭 . 𒀭𒈗 .
𒀭 . 𒈗 . 𒈗 . 𒈗 . 𒈗𒈗 𒈗𒈗 . 𒈗𒈗 . 𒀭 .

10

168. 𒀭 𒀀 . 𒁹 𒐊 . 𒄀 . 𒈗 . 𒐋 𒐊 . 𒐊 . 𒐋 𒐊 .

𒐊 𒐊 𒐊 . 𒁹 𒐊 . 𒐊 . 𒈗 . 𒁹 𒐊 𒐊 .

𒐊 𒐊 𒐊 .

169. 𒐊 𒐊 𒐊 . 𒐊 𒐊 𒐊 . 𒐊 . 𒐊 . 𒀸 . 𒁹 𒐊 .

𒐊 𒐊 . 𒈗 . 𒐊 𒐊 . 𒀸 . 𒐊 𒐊 .

NOTES.

159. " In my 30 campaigns " = " In my 30th campaign."

The city of Calkhi represents the Calah of Scripture.

cī utsbacuni " when I was stopping," 1st pers. sing. Permansive Kal of צב with conditional suffix *ni*.

Dayan-Assur, " Assur is judge," was the name of the Tartan (" strong chief ") or generalissimo.

160. 𒀭 𒀀 𒁹 (" host-many ") = " armies."

panat, pl. fem. construct of *pānu*.

umāhir " I urged on " (Heb. מהר).

The Upper Zab is here referred to.

161. *'ebir* " I crossed."

lib = " middle " (the heart being the middle of a thing).

Read *'alāni* from *alu* (Heb. אהל " tent "); the phonetic complement *ni* shows how the plural sign is to be read.

icdarrib, Iphteal of *carabu* " to approach " (Heb. קרב), *t* being changed into *d* after *c*.

mādātu = " tribute," literally " gift ;" for *mandattu* (*mandantu*), from *nadanu* (Heb. נתן).

162. *attakhar* " I received ;" Iphteal of מהר.

163. *attuśir* " I departed ;" Ittaphal of וסר, another form of *vassaru* " to leave " (Cp. Heb. מסר).

165. These are the Minni of the Old Testament.

    namurrat, fem. sing. construct from *namaru* " to see."

166. *iplakh* " he feared " (Aram. פלח).

    uvassir ; see line 163.

    suzub " the saying," Shaphel pass. verbal noun from עזב " to leave."

    napisti " life ; " the plural sign is not to be read in Assyrian.

    eli " he went up " from עלה.

167. *artedi*, Iphteal from רדה (Heb. ירד) " to descend."

    sāsu " spoil " (Cp. Heb. שסה).

    mani = " countable number." (Heb. מנה).

168. *abbal* " I strew down " (Heb. נפל).

    āgur for *aggur* " I dug up " (Heb. נקר).

    asrup " I burned " (Heb. שרף).

169. *limetu* from לוה " to cleave to."

    acsud " I took," with phonetic complement *ud.*